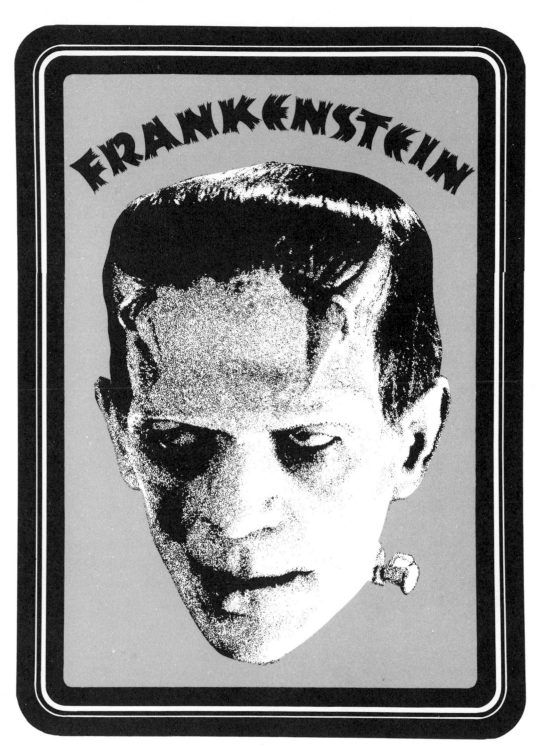

FRANKENSTEIN

Edited by Richard J. Anobile

UNIVERSE BOOKS

NEW YORK

A DARIEN HOUSE BOOK

UNIVERSE BOOKS
381 Park Avenue South
New York, N.Y. 10016

Library of Congress Catalogue Card Number: 74-77060

First Printing, March 1974.

ISBN 0 87663 207 X

Printed in the United States of America

Introduction

Following the success of DRACULA in 1931, Universal Pictures was anxious to find another film for its new star, Bela Lugosi. A young French-born director, Robert Florey, was then in Hollywood. He had been working on various talkies in New York and Paris, most notably the first Marx Brothers film, THE COCOANUTS. While lunching at the Musso & Frank Restaurant on Hollywood Boulevard, Florey was approached by his friend Richard Schayer, head of Universal's story department, who told him that the studio was searching for a story for a Lugosi film.

At a subsequent meeting Florey discussed several possibilities with Schayer: "The Invisible Man," "The Murders in the Rue Morgue," plays presented by the Théatre du Grand-Guignol de Paris, and Mary, Shelley's "Frankenstein," among others. There was an immediate agreement on the last of these, but more as a concept, using Shelley's story merely as the framework for the film. Shelley's monster was simply not the horrible creature Universal had in mind. Schayer suggested that Florey work on an outline for the film, one loosely based on the Shelley novel.

Florey set to work. Shelley's articulate creature was converted into a grunting monstrosity, the creation of a power-mad doctor. When Florey returned with his five page outline, Universal felt it had just what it wanted. But Florey refused to write a full screenplay until he was assured he could both write and direct for Universal. And this was the agreement they reached.

Florey was then joined by Garett Fort who wrote the dialogue from the story given him by Florey. It was for the part of the mad scientist, Dr. Henry Frankenstein, that Florey visualized Bela Lugosi. And it was only the concept of the scientist seeking to create new life from the remnants of dead bodies, which remained from the original novel. Florey was working in a small Los Angeles apartment over a Van de Kamp Bakery, whose well-known trademark is a rotating windmill; this spawned the idea for the final and fiery end of the monster.

Although pleased with Florey's script, Universal insisted that Lugosi be the monster, not its creator. Florey objected: It was a waste of talent to have Lugosi, a brilliant speaker, relegated to a role whose only lines would be grunts. But Carl Laemmle, then head of the studio, insisted that Lugosi was firmly established in the public's mind as a monster. Lugosi's studio contract read that he must play any role assigned him by Universal; if he refused, he could be barred from playing in any other films. Reluctantly, Florey and Lugosi went along with the wishes of Laemmle.

To better give the studio a feel of what the film would be like, Florey decided to shoot a two reel test on the old DRACULA castle set. He chose the creation sequence, probably the most dramatic part of the entire script. Paul Ivano was brought in as Florey's cinematographer and Jack Pierce developed the make-up for the monster. Aside from being reduced to playing a mumbling idiot, Lugosi was further annoyed by a two hour daily make-up ordeal to which he had to succumb.

While all this was going on, a new director found his way to Universal. He had made his reputation as a stage director and had three films to his credit: dialogue director for HELL'S ANGELS, and director of WATERLOO BRIDGE and of JOURNEY'S END. Universal was most pleased to have James Whale under contract. In line with other studios of the time, Universal felt it had to look to the stage for major film talent.

Whale was therefore given free reign and told to select the script which would be his first Universal film. He somehow got his hands on Florey's script of FRANKENSTEIN. His reaction was immediate and enthusiastic. Whale insisted that he, not Florey, direct this film. Universal was eager to please, and Florey was taken off the project. Florey ran to check his contract and discovered that, in fact, he was to both write and direct. But somehow the language of the contract did not make it clear that the film was to be FRANKENSTEIN and therefore, to avoid a lawsuit, the studio quickly assigned Florey to write and direct another Lugosi film, THE MURDERS IN THE RUE MORGUE. Lugosi was most pleased to shed the monster role, but Florey was justly angered.

Thus, Whale got his way and brought in someone

else to rewrite Florey's script. Action was sacrificed for more dialogue and the film went into production. And on its release, it was an immediate success.

Robert Florey was left with nothing of the success. His name had been removed as author of the screenplay. Only after Florey complained did his name go back in the credits of the film, but only on prints released in Europe; it was too late to add his name to the American release prints.

Repeated screenings of FRANKENSTEIN for this book, makes it difficult for one to understand why Universal thought it had a gem of a director in James Whale. His direction is primitive at best. The film is really shot as a stage play. Even the actors perform as if on stage, overgesturing to make their point clear to those in the very last rows and forgetting that the camera is the only 'audience' and it's always there front-center. Whale's background did not allow him to see how ludicrously the scenes between Colin Clive and Mae Clark actually played. Many lengthy and significant scenes are shot either as medium or long shots with Whale never giving the close-up any thought.

The only scene in which Whales exhibits any feeling for the medium was unfortunately mutilated by Universal. The pond scene in the released film shows the monster befriended by a young girl. She takes the monster by the hand, leads him to the pond and, to his delight and dismay, shows him that daisies thrown into the water will float. The monster is fascinated, but he soon runs out of flowers. He motions for the girl to come to him — and here ends the scene. Later we see the girl's father carrying her body amidst an aroused citizenry. The impression created is that the monster, in anger, perpetrated some truly 'monstrous' act and killed the girl in anger.

This is at odds with Whale's original scene and his intent. It was tender from the outset, with the monster clasping the girl's hands and examining them. He realizes, possibly for the first time, his own human origin. The original scene did not end with the monster motioning to the girl but continued as he tossed her into the pond, thinking she would float like the daisies. The girl screams and slowly sinks beneath the surface of the water. The monster, confused and disappointed, leaves.

From what I've been told the original scene was exhibited only in the previews of the film. Although Universal originally felt that the Shelley novel was not horrible enough for the type of film they had in mind, it apparently felt that *this* scene was too horrible. My attempts to secure some of this original footage to show some of the frame blow-ups in this introduction proved fruitless. I was told that if the studio wanted anyone to see the scene it would have been restored long ago, and further that the studio policy is probably no different today than it was in 1931. So much for the new sophistication of Hollywood. But in all probability, the scene no longer exists on film. It should be remembered that it was shot on nitrate stock — as was the entire film, and there would have been no reason for the studio to preserve the negative of that scene. Concrete evidence of the existence of the scene is the script continuity supplied to me by Universal. A continuity is taken from the film itself. The deleted scene can be found there.

Whale does seem to have come up with one innovation in FRANKENSTEIN. He allowed his camera to pan to characters other than the speaker and in some cases the speaker is off screen. While this is common practice today, this was most unusual at that time. Yet, based upon the completed film, one can only assume that any innovation Whale may have pioneered in FRANKENSTEIN was simply a matter of chance. His work does not exhibit a good knowledge of screen direction or film technique. And while one may argue that he was hampered by the lack of mobility of the early sound cameras, one could also point to more advanced uses of the sound camera prior to FRANKENSTEIN. One need only examine Florey's work on THE COCOANUTS, shot in 1929, to recognize Whale's deficiencies.

But, in spite of James Whale, FRANKENSTEIN is a classic and deservedly so.

Luckily Lugosi was unhappy with the role of the monster and even more fortuitous was Whale's acquaintance with an obscure stage actor named Henry Pratt, also known as Boris Karloff. Without the tremendous performance by Karloff, the premise of the film would never have been so terrifyingly conveyed to the audience. Though surrounded by mediocre, and sometimes laughable performances and stilted direction, Karloff manages to transcend what would normally be disastrous distractions for an audience. The monster is the only character in the film whose vivid personality remains with the reviewer. Though caked with several layers of make-up, Karloff's face manages to convey the full range of human emotions. His characterization established Karloff as a master of the horror genre and kept him in such roles throughout his life.

Karloff's sensitive performance constantly reminded the audience that they were seeing a creation whose origins were human. The monster is childlike and obviously relishes each new discovery, whether seeing light for the first time or experiencing a new found freedom beyond the castle door. His obvious fascination for life immediately places us on his side, and we find ourselves sharing his bewilderment as he discovers he is being destroyed.

Despite the static appearance of the film today, we can appreciate its classic theme — man playing God. It may be said that at a time of new and startling developments in medicine and technology, the film takes on an even greater relevance and is therefore the more terrifying by being all the more possible.

This book is a complete reconstruction of the film, from opening to closing credits. Every scene and just about every camera set-up are coupled with every word of dialogue to give you a permanent record of this film classic.

—Richard J. Anobile
New York City
February, 1974

Note to reader:

In keeping as true to the film as possible I have left in lap dissolves and fades where I felt they were necessary. The effect of a lap dissolve to the reader will be the appearance of two seemingly superimposed photos. The purpose here – as it was the director's, is to bridge the time and place gap between two scenes.

You will also notice a fuzziness in some frames. This is due to the fact that every photo is taken from blow-ups of the film itself. All possible means have been taken to insure clarity but inconsistencies in negative quality account for the variations of photo densities you will observe.

Acknowledgments

I would like to take this opportunity to thank those individuals and organizations whose cooperation have made this book possible.

The right to produce this book was granted to us by Universal Pictures; I would especially like to acknowledge the help of Steve Adler of that firm for his cooperation in seeing to it that all the necessary print materials were made available to me.

Alyne Model and George Norris of Riverside Film Associates transferred my marks to the negative material and attended to the details of that highly technical job. All the blow-ups were produced by Vita Print.

Harry Chester Associates was responsible for the design.

—Richard J. Anobile

Van Sloan: How do you do.

Van Sloan: Mr. Carl Laemmle feels that it would be a litle unkind to present this picture without just a word of friendly warning.

Van Sloan: We are about to unfold the story of Frankenstein, a man of science, who sought to create a man after his own image —

Van Sloan: Without reckoning upon God.

Van Sloan: It is one of the strangest tales ever told. It deals with the two great mysteries of creation. Life and death. I think it will thrill you.

Van Sloan: It may shock you . . . It might even — horrify you!

Van Sloan: So then, if you feel that you do not care to subject your nerves to such a strain.

Van Sloan: Now is your chance to — well — well — we've warned you!

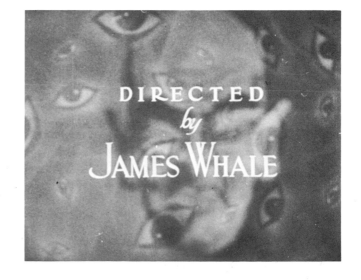

THE PLAYERS

Henry Frankenstein ... COLIN CLIVE
Elizabeth .... MAE CLARKE
Victor Moritz .... JOHN BOLES
The Monster .... ?
Doctor Waldman .. EDWARD VAN SLOAN
Baron Frankenstein .... FREDERICK KERR
Fritz .... DWIGHT FRYE
The Burgomaster .... LIONEL BELMORE
Little Maria .... MARILYN HARRIS

Frankenstein: Down . . . down, you fool . . . . !

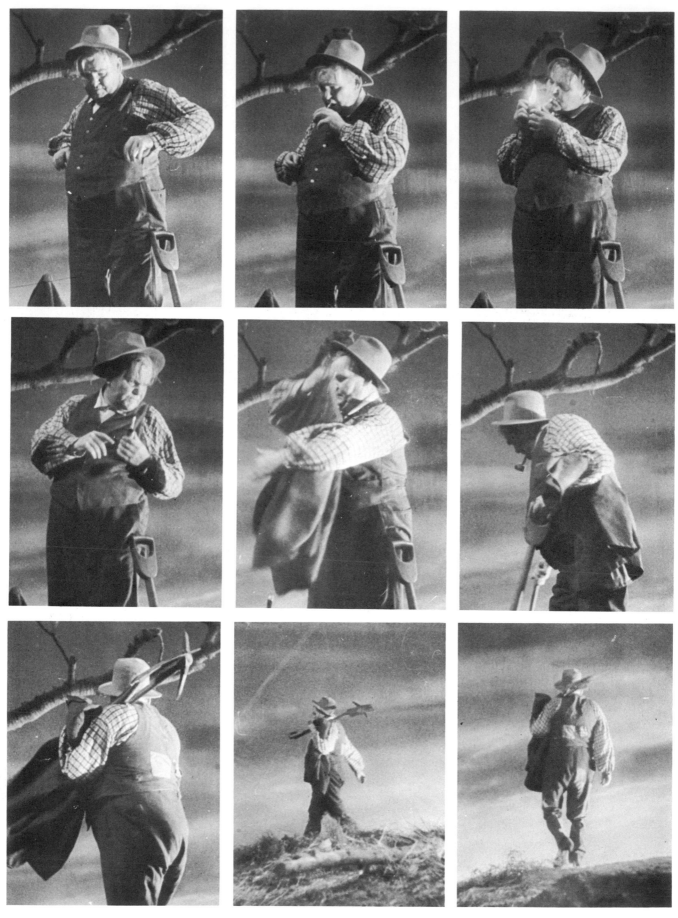

Frankenstein: Now . . . come on.

Frankenstein: Hurry . . . hurry . . .

Frankenstein: The moon's rising . . . we've no time
to lose!

Frankenstein: Careful!

Fritz: Here he comes!

Frankenstein: He is just resting, waiting for a new life to come.

Frankenstein: Here we are.

Frankenstein: Look. It's still here.

Frankenstein: Climb up and cut the rope.

Fritz: Nooo!

Frankenstein: Go on. It can't hurt you.
Here's the knife.

Fritz: Look out!

Fritz: Here I come!

Fritz: Is it all right?

Frankenstein: The neck's broken, the brain is useless.

Frankenstein: We must find another brain.

Dr. Waldman: That will do, gentlemen . . .

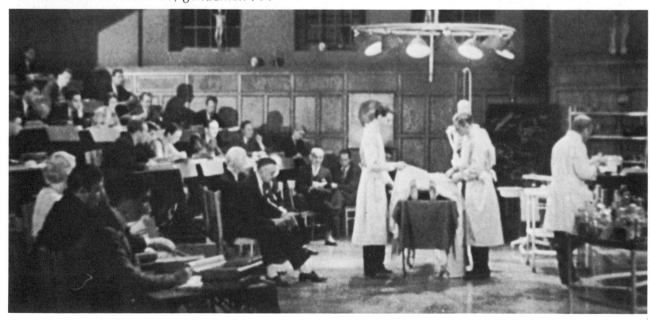

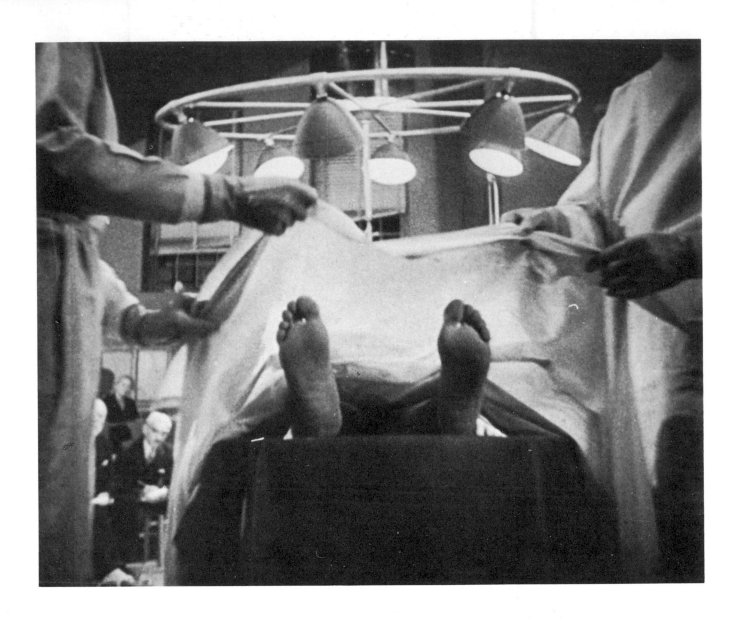

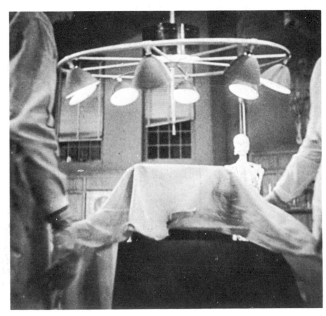
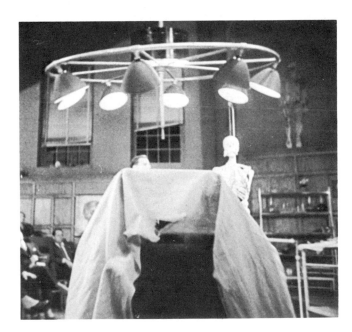

Dr. Waldman: And in conclusion, ladies and gentlemen —

Dr. Waldman: Here we have one of the most perfect specimens . . .

Dr. Waldman: . . . of the human brain that has ever come to my attention at the University.

Dr. Waldman: And here the abnormal brain of the typical criminal.

Dr. Waldman: Observe, ladies and gentlemen, the scarcity of convolutions on the frontal lobe —

Dr. Waldman: As compared to that of the normal brain.

Dr. Waldman: . . . and the distinct degeneration of the middle frontal lobe —

Dr. Waldman: All of the degenerate characteristics check amazingly with the history of the dead man before us whose —

Dr. Waldman: Life was one of brutality, of violence and murder.

Dr. Waldman: Both of these jars will remain here for your further inspection.

Dr. Waldman: Thank you, gentlemen, the class is dismissed.

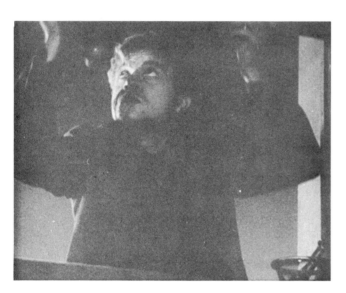

 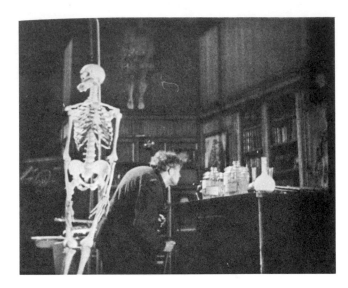

 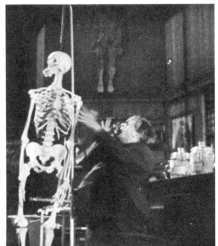 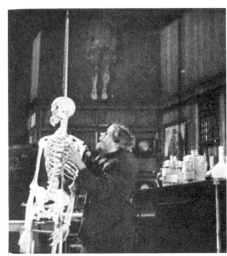

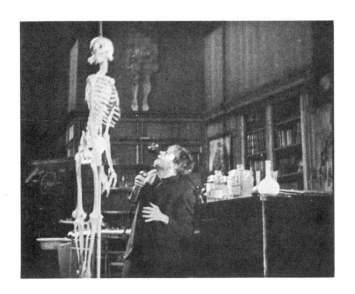 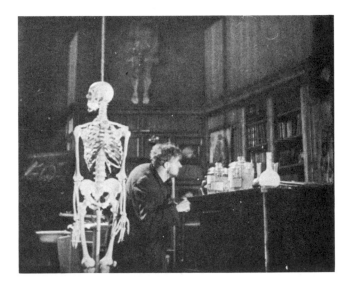

Maid: Herr Victor Moritz.

Elizabeth: Victor! I'm so glad you've come.

Victor: What is it, Elizabeth?

Victor: Oh, you've heard from Henry.
Elizabeth: Yes. The first word in four months. It just came, Victor, you must help me.

Victor: Why, of course I'll help you.

Elizabeth: I'm afraid. I've read this over and over again but they're just words that I can't understand. Listen.

Elizabeth: "You must have faith in me, Elizabeth. Wait. My work must come first, even before you. At night the winds howl in the mountains — there is no one here. Prying eyes can't peer into my secret."

Elizabeth: What can he mean?

Victor: What does he say then?

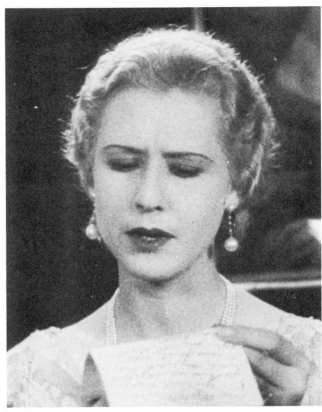

Elizabeth: "I am living in an abandoned old watch tower close to the town of Goldstadt. Only my assistant is here to help me with my experiments."

Victor: Oh, his experiments!

Elizabeth: Yes, that's what frightens me. The very day we announced our engagement he told me of his experiments. He said he was on the verge of a discovery so terrific that he doubted his own sanity.

Elizabeth: There was a strange look in his eyes — some mystery — his words carried me right away. Of course, I've never doubted him, but —

Elizabeth: Still I worry. I can't help it. And now this letter.

Elizabeth: Oh, this uncertainty can't go on. I must know. Victor, have you seen him?
Victor: Yes, about three weeks ago.

Victor: I met him walking alone in the woods. He spoke to me of his work, too.

Victor: I asked him if I might visit his laboratory. He glared at me and said he would let *no one* go there. His manner was very strange.

Elizabeth: Oh, what can we do! Oh, if he should be ill.

Victor: Now don't worry. I'll go to Doctor Waldman, Henry's old professor at Medical School.

Victor: Perhaps he can tell us more about all this.

Elizabeth: Victor, you're a dear.
Victor: You know I'd go to the ends of the earth for you.

Elizabeth: But I shouldn't like that. I'm far too fond of you.

Victor: I wish you were.

Elizabeth: Victor!
Victor: I'm sorry.

Elizabeth: Good night, Victor, and thank you. Thank you.

48

Victor: Good night and don't worry. You promise?
Elizabeth: I won't.

Elizabeth: Victor!

Victor: What is it?
Elizabeth: I'm coming with you.

Victor: But Elizabeth, you can't do that!
Elizabeth: I must! I'll be ready in a minute.

Dr. Waldman: Herr Frankenstein is a most brilliant young man, yet so erratic, he troubles me.
Elizabeth: I'm worried about Henry. Why has he left the University? He was doing so well and he seemed so happy with his work.

Dr. Waldman: Well, you know, his researches in the field of chemical galvanism and electro biology were far in advance of our theories here at the University. In fact, he had reached a most advanced stage. They were becoming dangerous.

Dr. Waldman: Herr Frankenstein is greatly changed.
Victor: You mean changed as a result of his work?
Dr. Waldman: Yes, his work, his insane ambition to create life.
Elizabeth: How? How? Please tell us everything — whatever it is.

Dr. Waldman: The bodies we use in our lecture room for dissecting purposes were not perfect enough for his experiments. He wished us to supply him with other bodies and we were not to be too particular as to where and how we got them.

Dr. Waldman: I told him that his demands were unreasonable and so he left the University to work unhampered. He found what he needed elsewhere.

Victor: Oh! The bodies of animals, well, what are the lives of a few rabbits and dogs.

Dr. Waldman: You do not quite get what I mean. Herr Frankenstein was interested only in human life. First to destroy it and then re-create it. There you have his mad dream.

Elizabeth: Can we go to him?
Dr. Waldman: You will not be very welcome.
Elizabeth: Oh, what does that matter! I must see him.

Elizabeth: Dr. Waldman, you have influence with Henry. Won't you come with us?
Dr. Waldman: I'm sorry, but Herr Frankenstein is no longer my pupil.

Elizabeth: But he respects you. Won't you help us to take him away?
Dr. Waldman: Very well, Fraulein, I have warned you, but if you wish it I will go.

Frankenstein: Fritz.
Fritz: Hello!

Frankenstein: Have you finished making those connections?

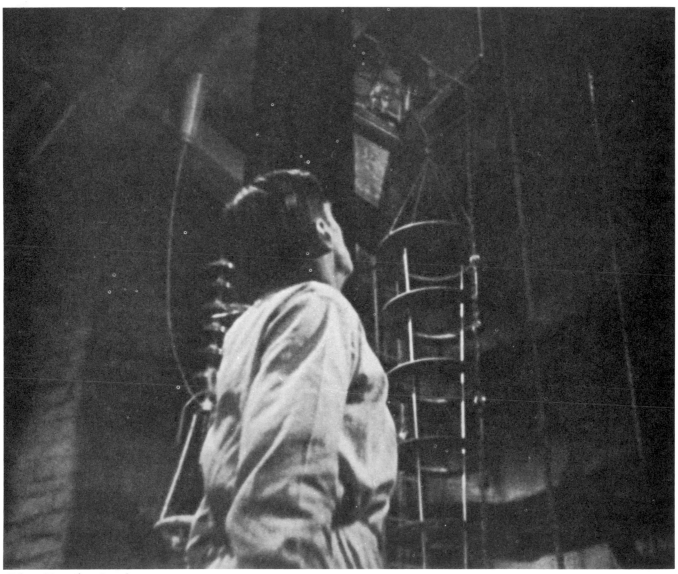

Fritz: Yes, they're done.
Frankenstein: Well, come down then and help with these attachments. We've lots to do.

Fritz: Look out!

Frankenstein: Fool! If this storm developes as I hope you'll have plenty to be afraid of before the night is over. Go on! Fix the electrodes!

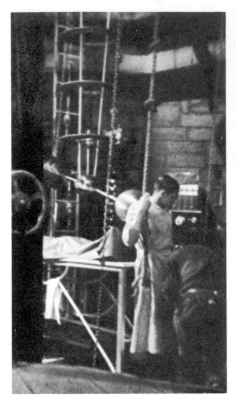

Frankenstein: This storm will be magnificent — All the electrical secrets of Heaven!

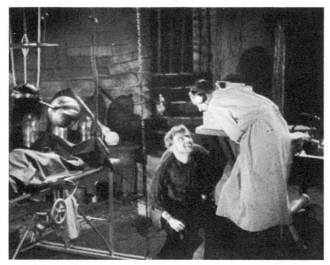

Frankenstein: And this time we're ready, eh Fritz? Ready!

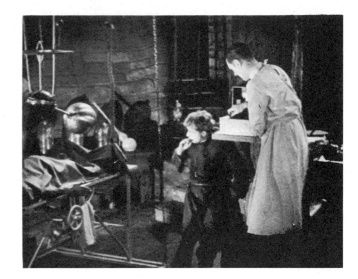

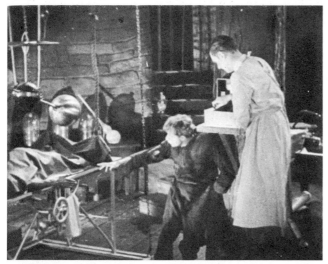

Fritz: Oh!

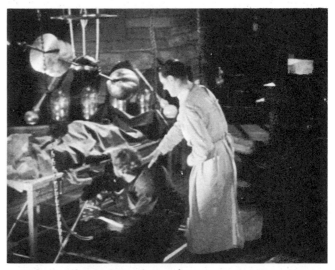

Frankenstein: Why, what's the matter?
Fritz: Look!

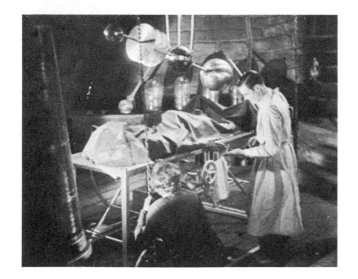

Frankenstein: There's nothing to fear. Look —

Frankenstein: No blood, no decay. Just a few stitches — And look.

Frankenstein: Here's the final touch.

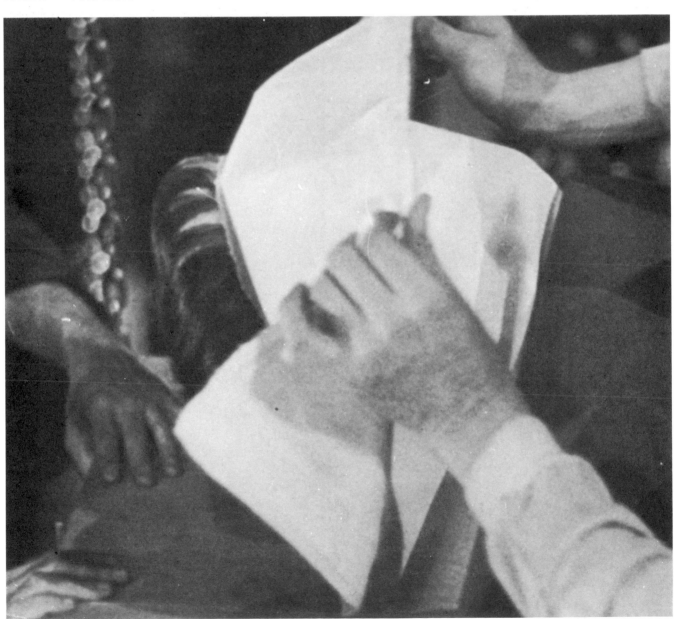

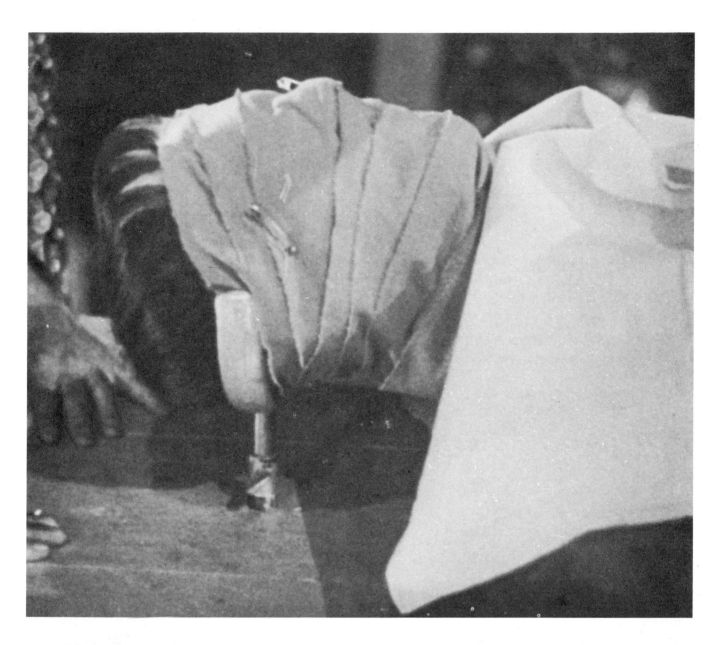

Frankenstein: The brain you stole, Fritz. Think of it!

Frankenstein: The brain of a dead man waiting to live again in a body I made with my own hands!

Frankenstein! With my own hands!

Frankenstein: Let's have one final test. Throw the switches.

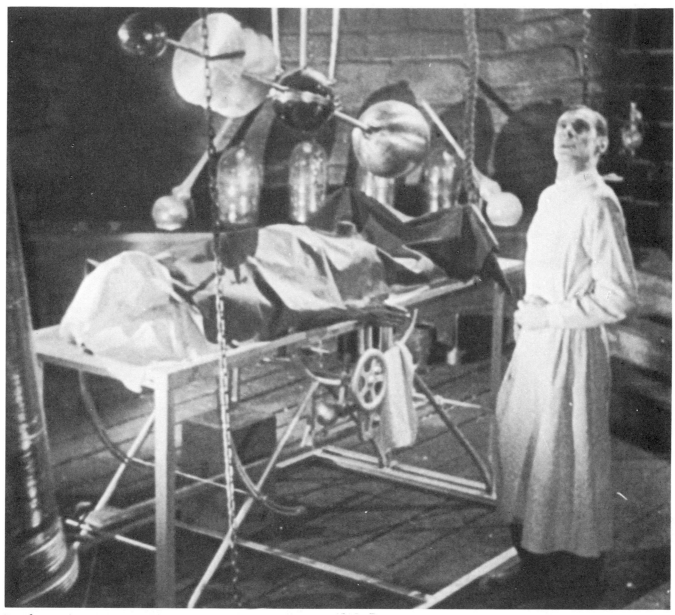

Frankenstein: Good! In fifteen minutes the storm should be at its height. Then we'll be ready.

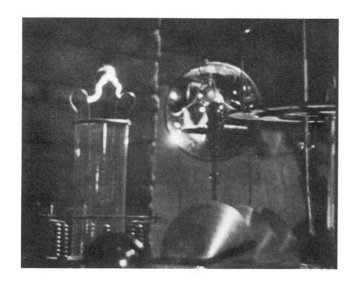

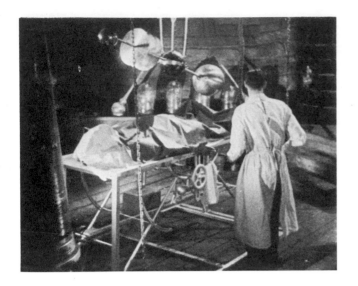

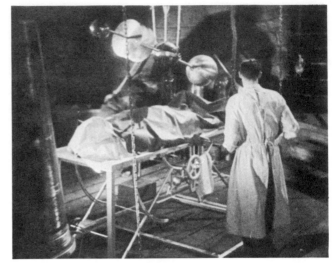

Franknstein: What's that?

Fritz: There's someone there.

Frankenstein: Quiet.

Frankenstein: Send them away! Nobody must come here.

Frankenstein: Here! Cover this!

Frankenstein: Whoever it is don't let them in.
Fritz: Leave them to me.

Frankenstein: Of all times for anybody to come! Now!

Fritz: Think I'm going to let these people in? Not much. Can't have people messing about at this time of night. Got too much to do.

Fritz: Wait a minute! All right! All right!

Dr. Waldman: It's Dr. Waldman, Fritz.
Fritz: You can't see him. Go away!

Fritz: All right, Doctor —
you can't get in!

Victor: Henry!
Dr. Waldman: Herr Frankenstein!
Elizabeth: Henry!

Frankenstein: Who is it? Who is it? What do you want? You must leave me alone now!
Elizabeth: It's Elizabeth! Open the door!

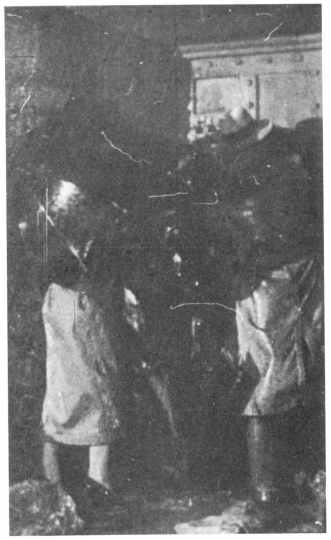

Victor: Henry!
Dr. Waldman: Frankenstein!
Victor: Henry!
Elizabeth: Open the door!
Dr. Waldman: Let us in!

Elizabeth: Henry!
Doctor: Frankenstein!
Victor: Henry!

Frankenstein: What do you want?
Elizabeth: Open the door.
Doctor: Let us in.

Frankenstein: You must leave me alone.
Elizabeth: Well Henry, at least give us shelter.

Victor: What's all this nonsense of locked doors?

Elizabeth: Henry!
Frankenstein: Elizabeth, please. Won't you go away. Won't you trust me just for tonight?

Elizabeth: You're ill. What's the matter?
Frankenstein: Nothing.

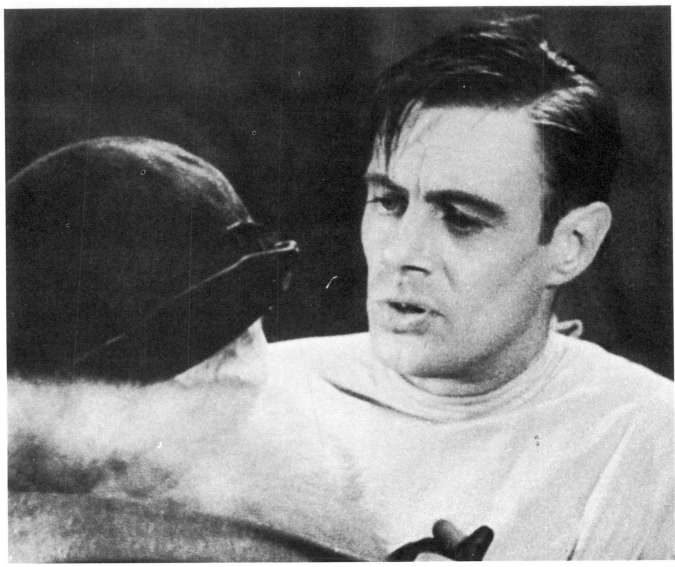

Frankenstein: I'm quite all right. Truly I am. Oh can't you see I mustn't be disturbed? You'll ruin everything. My experiment is almost completed.

Elizabeth: Wait a moment. I understand. I I believe in you. But I can *not* leave you tonight.

Frankenstein: You've got to leave!

Victor: Henry, you're inhuman!

Victor: You're crazy!

Frankenstein: Crazy am I? You'll see whether I'm crazy or not. Come on up.

Frankenstein: Are you quite sure you want to come in?

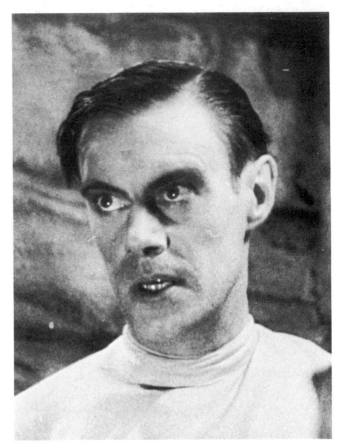
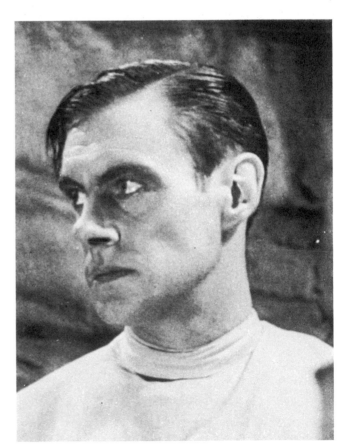

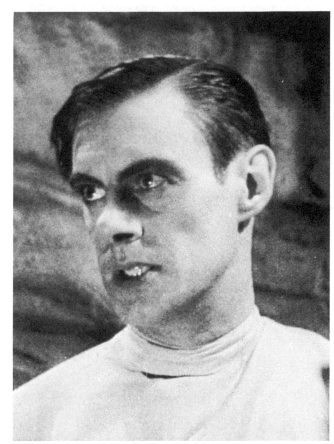

Frankenstein: Very well.

Frankenstein: Forgive me — but I'm forced to take unusual precautions.

Frankenstein: Sit down, please.

Frankenstein: Sit down!

Frankenstein: You too, Elizabeth. Please.

Frankenstein: A moment ago you said I was crazy. Tomorrow we'll see about that.

Fritz: Don't touch that!

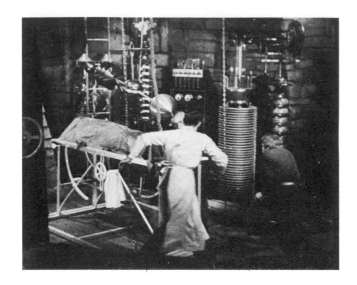

Frankenstein: I'm sorry, Doctor, but I insist.

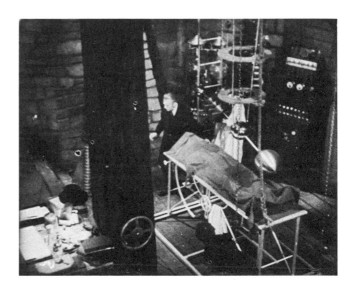

Frankenstein: Please.

Frankenstein: Dr. Waldman, I learned a great deal from you at the University about the violet ray, the ultraviolet ray which you said was the highest color in the spectrum.

Frankenstein: You were wrong. Here in this machinery I have gone beyond that.

Frankenstein: I have discovered the great ray that first bought life into the world.

Frankenstein: Tonight you shall have the proof. At first I experimented only with dead animals . . . and then a human heart which I kept beating for three weeks. But now I am going to turn that ray on that body and endow it with life!

Dr. Waldman: And you really believe that you can bring life to the dead?

Frankenstein: That body is not dead.

Frankenstein: It has never lived! I created it!

Frankenstein: Dead, eh?

Frankenstein: I made it with my own hands from the bodies I took from the graves, from the gallows, anywhere!

Frankenstein: Go and see for yourself.

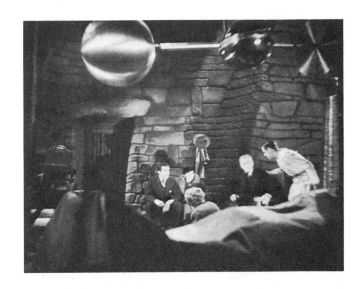

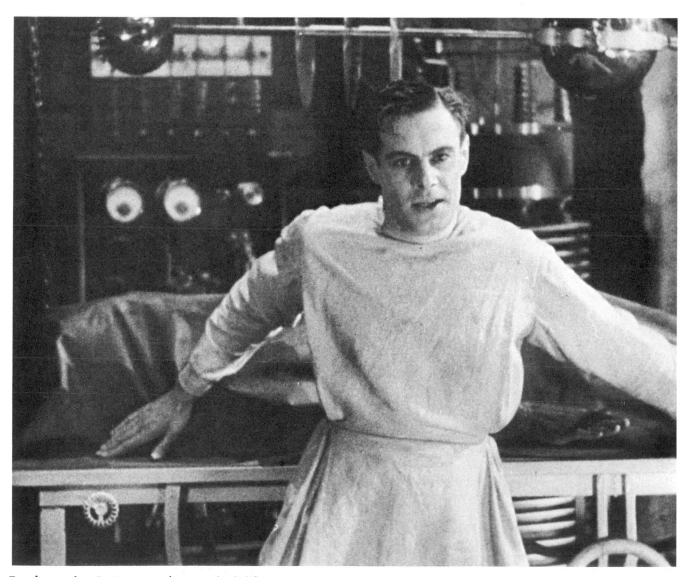

Frankenstein: Quite a good scene, isn't it?

Frankenstein: One man crazy —

Frankenstein: And three very sane spectators.

Frankenstein: Is everything ready?
Fritz: Yes.

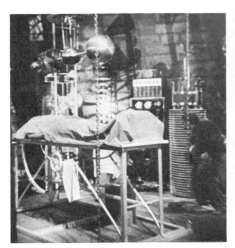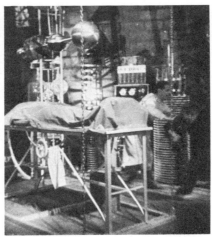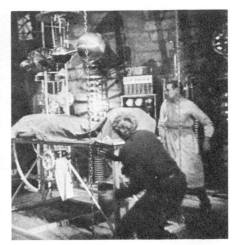

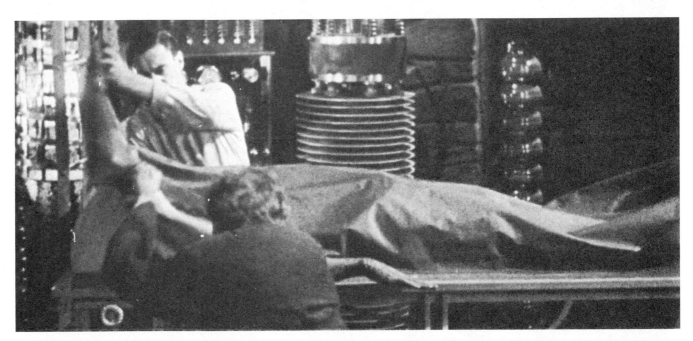

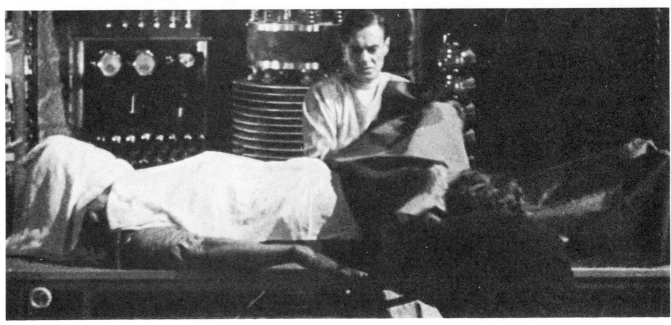

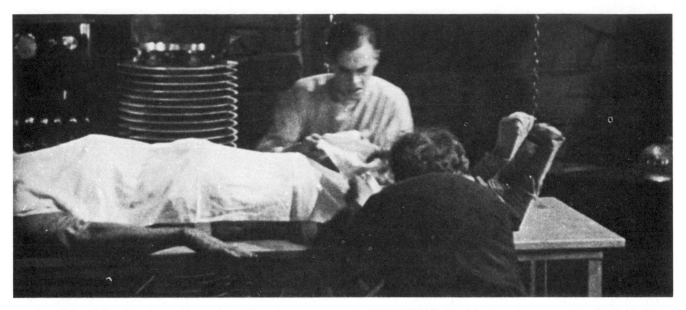

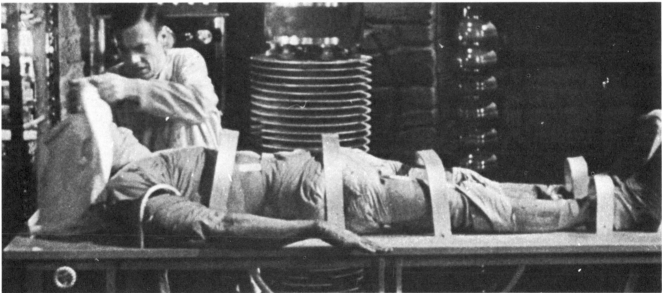

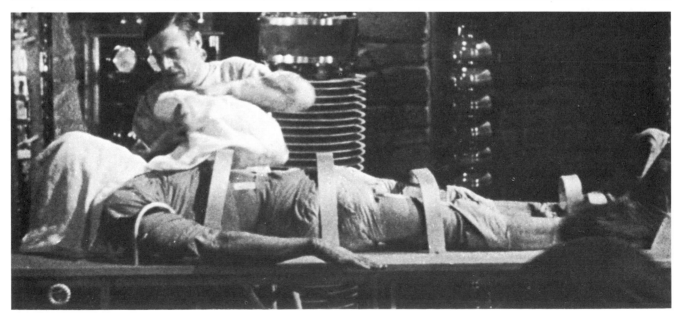

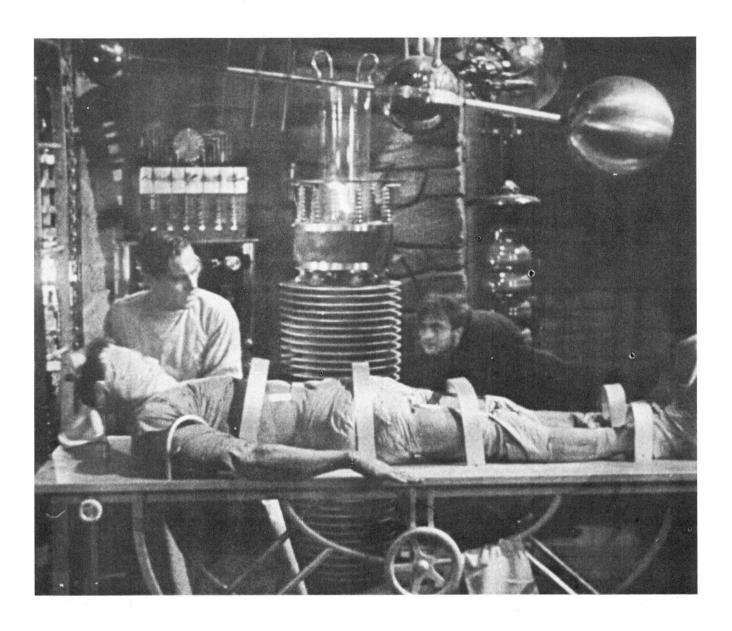

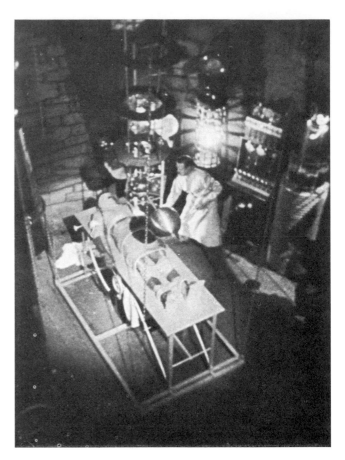

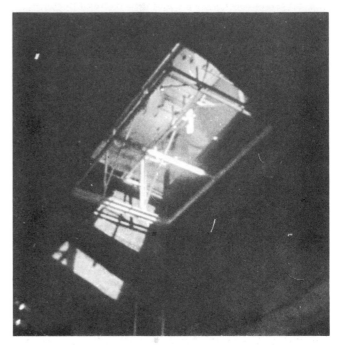

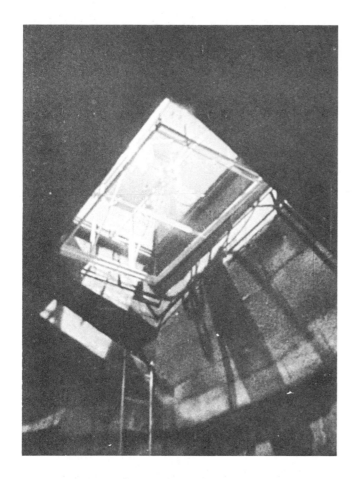

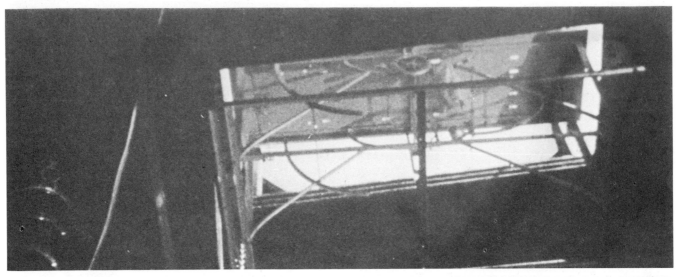

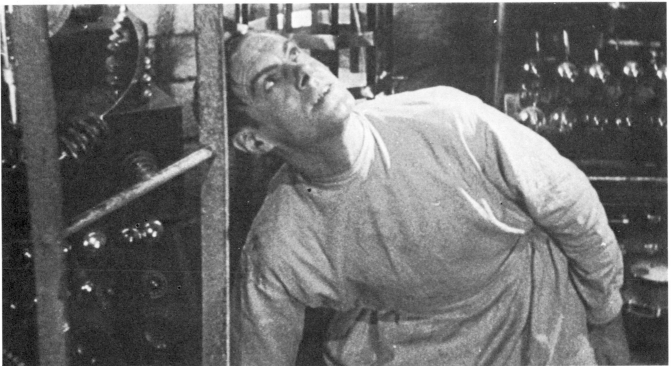

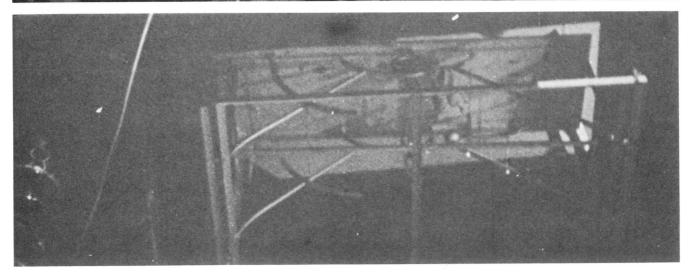

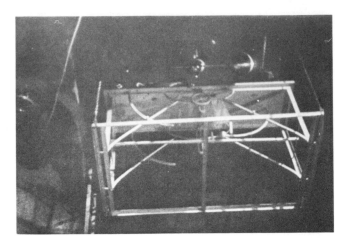
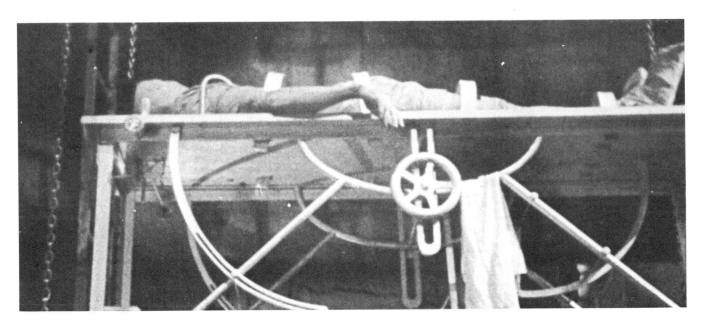
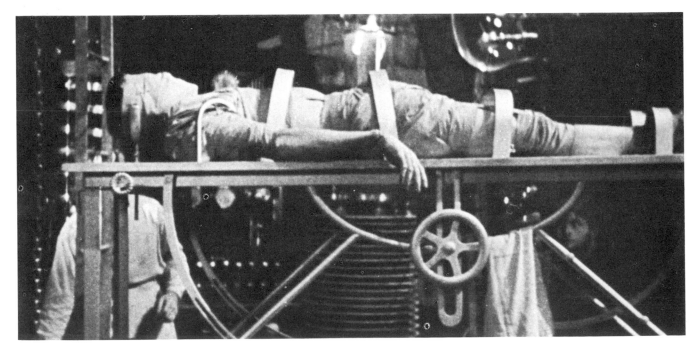

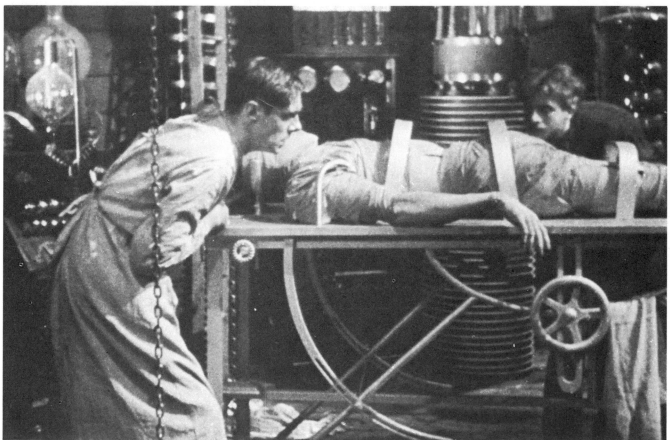

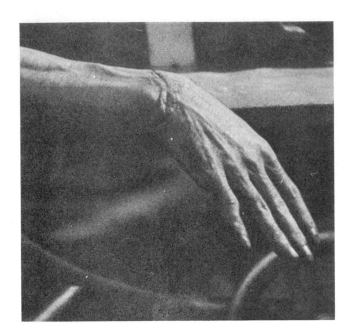

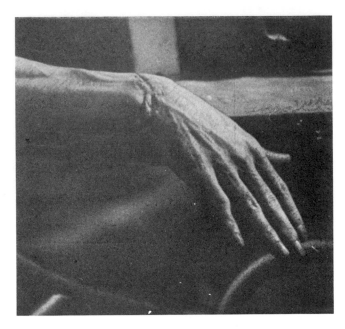

Frankenstein: It's moving — it's alive —

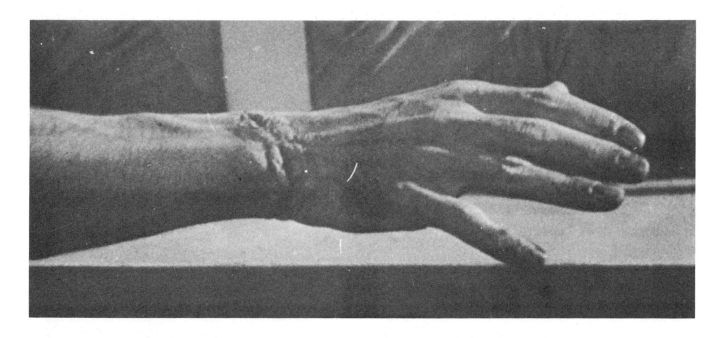

Frankenstein: It's alive — it's alive!

Frankenstein: It's alive — it's alive — it's alive.

Frankenstein: IT'S ALIVE! IT'S ALIVE!

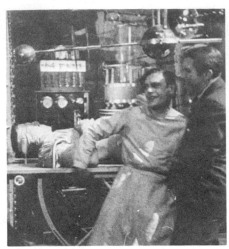 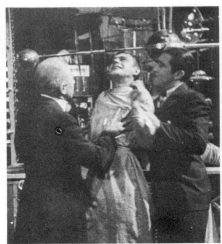 

Victor: Henry —in the name of God! **Frankenstein:** Oh — In the name of God. Now I know what it feels like to be God!

Victor: Henry is well but he is very busy. He said he would get in touch with you soon.
Elizabeth: Don't worry about him, Baron. He'll be home in a few days.

Baron: You two have it all arranged, haven't you? You think I'm an idiot, don't you? But I'm not.

Baron: Anyone can see with half an eye that there's something wrong. And I have two eyes and pretty good ones at that. Well, what is it?

Victor: You're quite mistaken, Baron.
Baron: What's the matter with my son? What's he doing?
Elizabeth: He's completing his experiments. That's all.

Baron: Why does he go messing around in an old ruined windmill when he has a decent house, a bath, good food and drink and a darned pretty girl to come back to — huh! Will you tell me that?
Elizabeth: Baron, you don't understand.

Baron: I understand perfectly well — huh — there is another woman, and you're afraid to tell me. Pretty sort of experiments these must be! Huh!

Elizabeth: Oh, but you're wrong!
Baron: Well, how do you know? Huh?
Maid: If you please Herr Baron — the Burgomaster.

Baron: Well, tell him to go away!
Maid: But he says it's important.

Baron: Nothing the Burgomaster can say can be of the slightest importance!

Burgomaster: Good day, Herr Baron.
Baron: Eh!

Burgomaster: Fraulein!

Baron: Well, what do you want? If it's trouble, go away — I've trouble enough.

Burgomaster: Oh, there's no trouble sir!

Baron: What do you mean, no trouble? There's nothing but trouble!

Burgomaster: I brought you these flowers.
Elizabeth: Thank you, Herr Vogel.

Burgomaster: Both in my private and official capacities as Burgomaster . . .

Baron: Yes, yes, yes, yes, we know all about that, but what do you want?
Burgomaster: Well —

Burgomaster: Well what I really want to know is, when will the wedding be, if you please?

Baron: Huh! Unless Henry comes to his senses, there'll be no wedding at all.

Burgomaster: But, Herr Baron, the village is already prepared!
Baron: Well tell them to unprepare!

Burgomaster: Oh, but such a lovely bride. Such a fine young man, the image of his father!
Baron: Heaven forbid!
Burgomaster: But sir, everything is ready.

Baron: I know that. Don't keep on saying so, you idiot! Th . . th . . there is nothing to cry about.

Burgomaster: Good day, Miss Elizabeth. Good day, Herr. Moritz.

Burgomaster: Good day, Herr Baron! **Baron:** Good day, Herr Vogel.

Baron: And good riddance to you! There you are! Huh! You see how it is! The whole village is kept waiting. The bride is kept waiting. And I am kept waiting!

Baron: Henry must come if I have to fetch him myself!

Victor: No, no, Baron!
Baron: What do you mean, no, no?

Victor: What about his work?
Baron: Stuff and nonsense! What about his wedding!

Baron: There is another woman and I'm going to find her!

Frankenstein: Oh, come and sit down, doctor, you must be patient . . . do you expect perfection at once?

Dr. Waldman: This creature of yours should be kept under guard! Mark my words, he will prove dangerous!

Frankenstein: Dangerous! Poor old Waldman. Have you never wanted to do anything that was dangerous?

Frankenstein: Where should we be if nobody tried to find out what lies beyond?

Frankenstein: Have you never wanted to look beyond the clouds and the stars or to know what causes the trees to bud? And what changes darkness into light?

Frankenstein: But if you talk like that, people call you crazy.

Frankenstein: Well, if I could discover just one of these things, what eternity is, for example. I wouldn't care if they did think I was crazy!

Doctor: You're young, my friend. Your success has intoxicated you. Wake up and look facts in the face. Here we have a fiend whose brain —

Frankenstein: Whose brain must be given time to develop. It's a perfectly good brain, doctor. Well, you ought to know, it came from your own laboratory . . .

Doctor: The brain that was stolen from my laboratory was a criminal brain.

Frankenstein: Oh, well, after all it's only a piece of dead tissue.

Dr. Waldman: Only evil can come of it. Your health will be ruined if you persist in this madness!

Frankenstein: I'm astonishingly sane, Doctor. . . .
Dr. Waldman: You have created a monster and it will destroy you!
Frankenstein: Patience. Patience. I believe in this monster as you call it. And if you don't, well, you must leave me alone . . .

Dr. Waldman: But think of Elizabeth, your father.
Frankenstein: Elizabeth believes in me, my father never believes in anyone. I've got to experiment further.

Frankenstein: He's only a few days old, remember, so far he's been kept in complete darkness. wait 'till I bring him into the light!

Frankenstein: Here he comes. Let's turn out the lights.

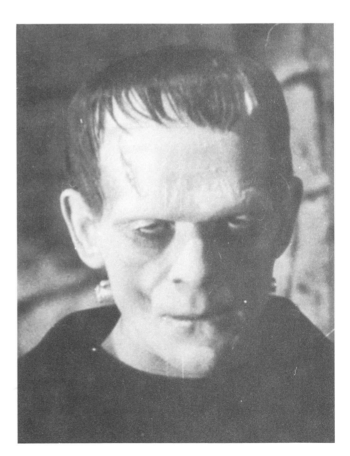

Frankenstein: Come in, come in,

Frankenstein: Sit down!

Frankenstein: Sit down.

Frankenstein: You see, it understands. Watch!

Dr. Waldman: Shut out the light!

Frankenstein: Sit down.

Frankenstein: Go and sit down!

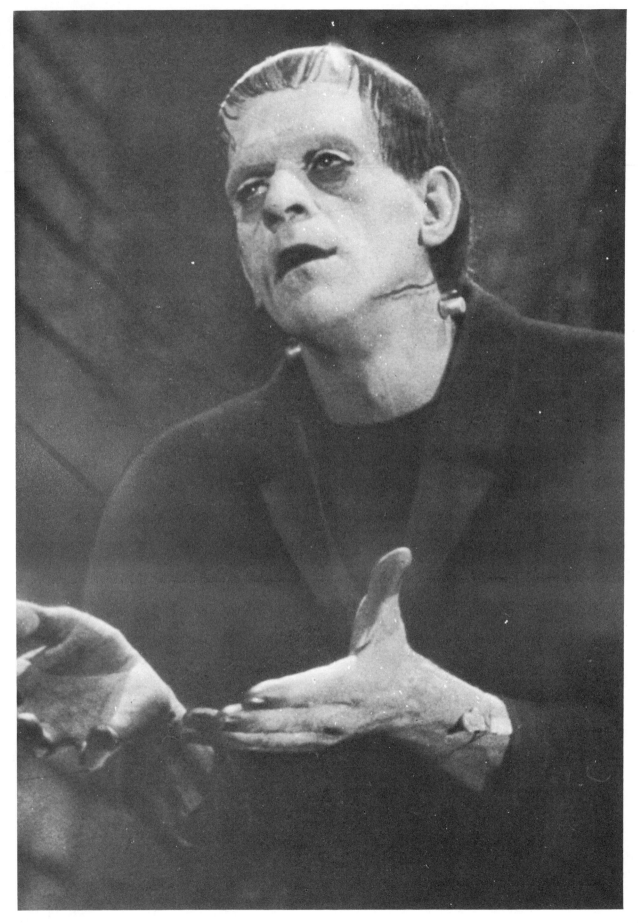

Frankenstein: It understands this time. It's wonderful!

Fritz: Frankenstein, Frankenstein! Where is he? Where is he? . . .

Frankenstein: Put that thing out, you fool! . . .

Frankenstein: Get away with that torch!

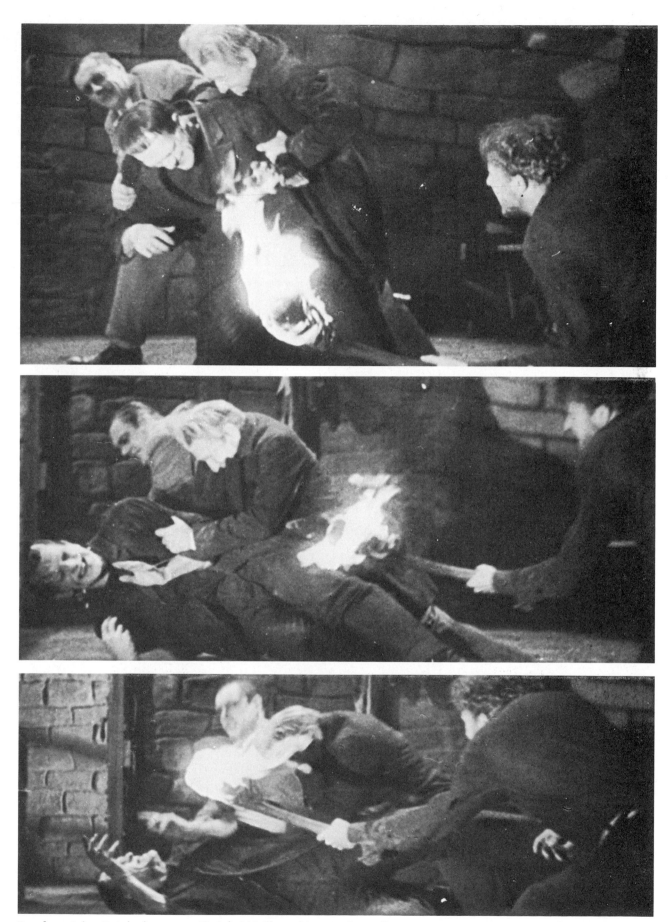

Frankenstein: Fetch the rope. Quick, We'll get him to the cellar!

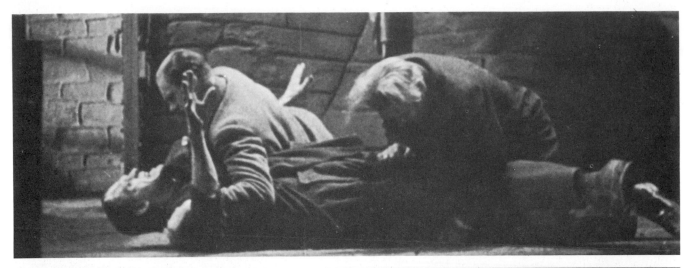

Frankenstein: Get away . . . he has the strength of ten men!

Fritz: Quiet. . . . quiet!
Frankenstein: Stop that! You will have the whole countryside on us.

Frankenstein: Back! Here give me that!

Frankenstein: Oh, come away, Fritz. Just leave it alone. Leave it alone!

Fritz: Ha! . . . Here's fire for you!

Frankenstein: Listen, what's that?

Frankenstein: It's Fritz. . . Come on, doctor, quick, hurry!

Frankenstein: Get back. . . .

Dr. Waldman: Back. . . quick . . . quick!

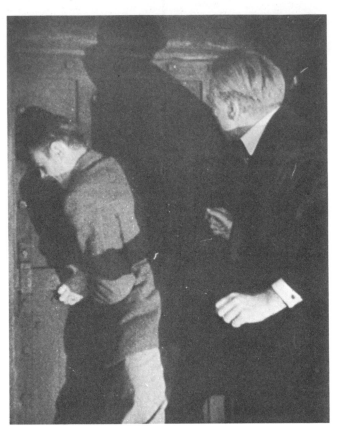

Frankenstein: He hated Fritz. Fritz always
tormented him.

Dr. Waldman: Come, come, pull yourself together!
Frankenstein: What can we do?

Dr. Waldman: Kill it, as you would any savage animal. We must overpower him first. Get me a hypodermic needle.

Frankenstein: It's murder!
Dr. Waldman: It's our only chance! In a few minutes he'll be through that door.

Dr. Waldman: Come, quick . . . hurry!

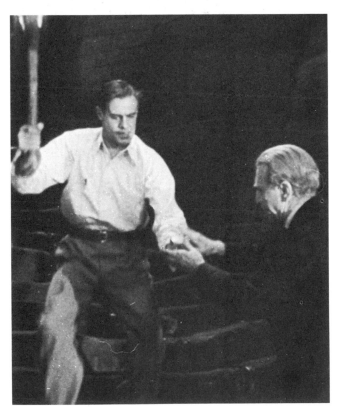

Dr. Waldman: Have you got it?
Frankenstein: Yes, here it is. It's very strong —
half grain solution.

Dr. Waldman: Good. Now then, now you stand there. When he goes toward you . . .

Dr. Waldman: I will make an injection in his back — ready?

Frankenstein: Yes.

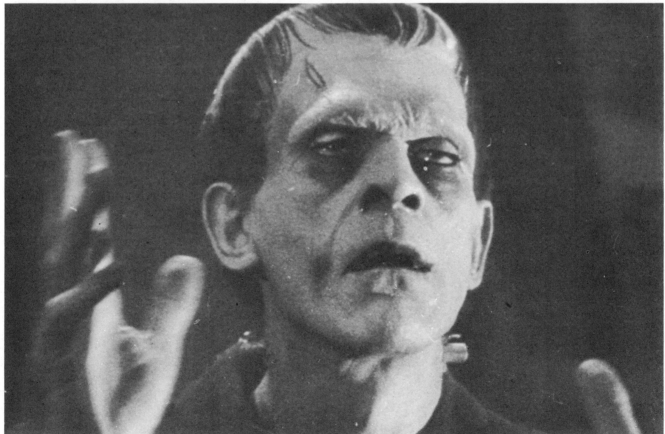

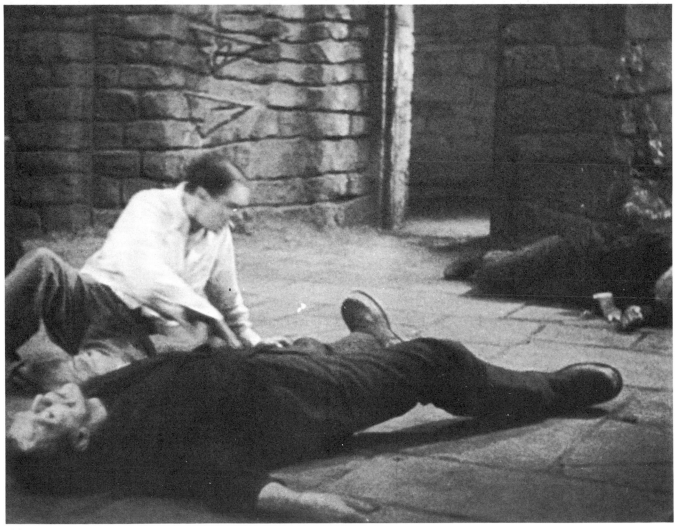

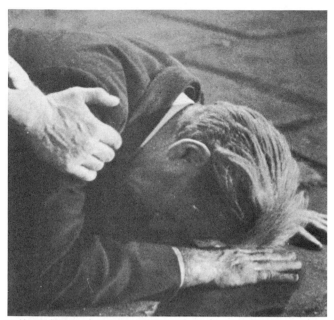

Frankenstein: Doctor Waldman . . . Dr. Waldman. Are you hurt?

Dr. Waldman: No . . . no, I am all right, it is nothing. See who is at the door . . .

Victor: What's happening here? Elizabeth and your father are coming up the hill to see you.

Frankenstein: You must keep them out.
Victor: It's too late!

Dr. Waldman: They must not see that here.
Quick, give me a hand . . .

Dr. Waldman: Have you got it?

Dr. Waldman: Henry, you'd better hurry upstairs and get that blood off your face before your father and Elizabeth get here.

Baron: There doesn't seem to be anybody in the place.

Baron: Oh!

Baron: There — there! What a — what a forsaken place!

Baron: Are you trying to burn it down hey what? What for, heh?

Baron: What's the matter with you? You look as though you'd been kicked by a horse. Where's Henry?

Victor: He can't be disturbed just now.
Baron: Oh, can't he? Huh! I'll soon settle that nonsense.

Elizabeth: Victor, where is he?
Baron: This place seems to drive everybody crazy. Henry — What — what's that?

Dr. Waldman: I — I beg your pardon. I am Dr. Waldman.
Baron: Oh, are you? I'm Baron Frankenstein.

Baron: Perhaps — perhaps you know what all this tommyrot's about. I'll be shot if I do.
Dr. Waldman: I would advise you to take Henry away from here at once!

Baron: Well, what do you suppose I'm here for? Pleasure? Huh! No!

Baron: Where are you, my dear?

Baron: Oh, there you are. Let's go and see what's up these awful stairs.

Baron: I don't know how in the deuce I'm going to get up them. Now, just watch me do the trick.
Dr. Waldman: Leave them alone.

Baron: No banisters or anything else. **Elizabeth:** Henry! **Frankenstein:** Elizabeth.
Frankenstein: Come in.

Elizabeth: Henry! Victor! Dr. Waldman! Come quickly!

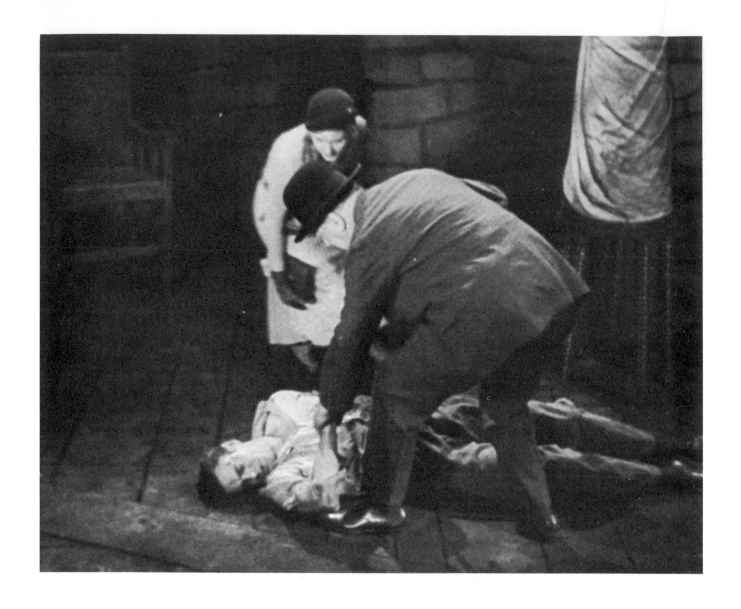

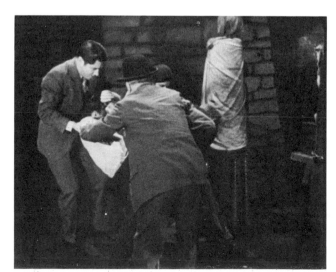

Frankenstein: Poor Fritz.
Elizabeth: Oh Henry, what have they done to you!

Frenkenstein: Poor Fritz! And it's all my fault!
Baron: Oh, my boy — get him onto the sofa.

144

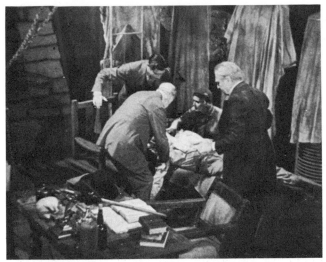

Frankenstein: Oh, my poor Fritz! Thank you — oh!
Victor: Got any brandy?

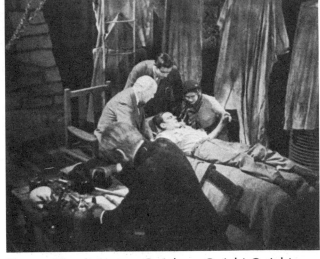

Baron: Give it to me. Quick — Quick! Quick!

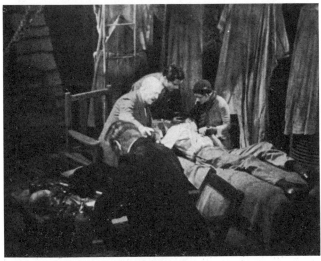

Baron: Here — I'll do that. Here, my boy.

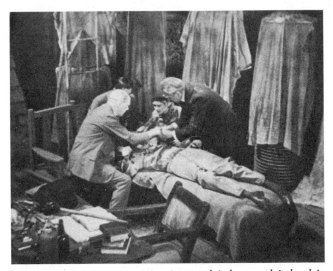

Baron: Now, now, now, now drink — drink this.

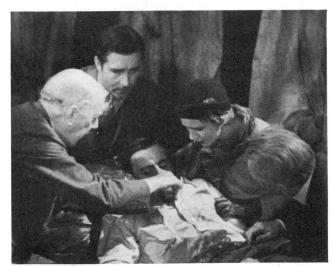

Baron: There — there, that's better. I'm going to take you home with me, Henry.

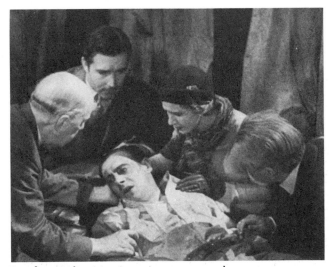

Frankenstein: No, I can't — my work.

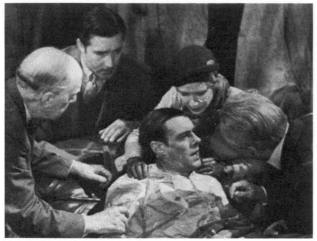

Frankenstein: What would happen to the records of my experiment?
Dr. Waldman: We will preserve them and, Henry —

Dr. Waldman: I will see that it is painlessly destroyed.
Frankenstein: Oh, Doctor —
Dr. Waldman: Yes, yes, leave it all to me.

Frankenstein: Oh, poor Fritz! Oh, my poor Fritz! All my fault!

Elizabeth: Henry, you can't do any more now. You must come home until you get well again. You'll soon feel better when you get out of here.

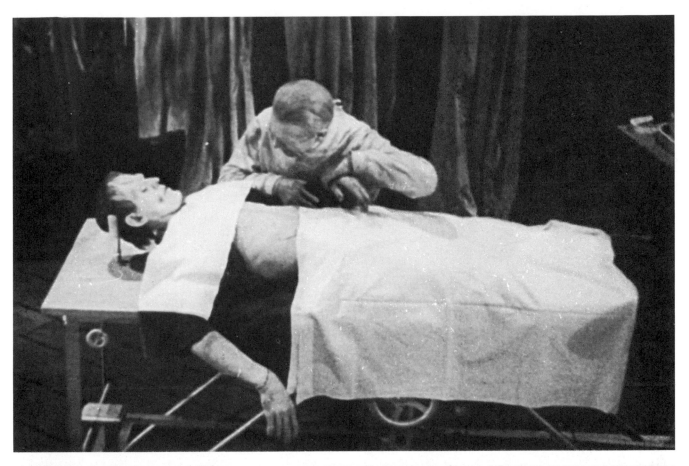

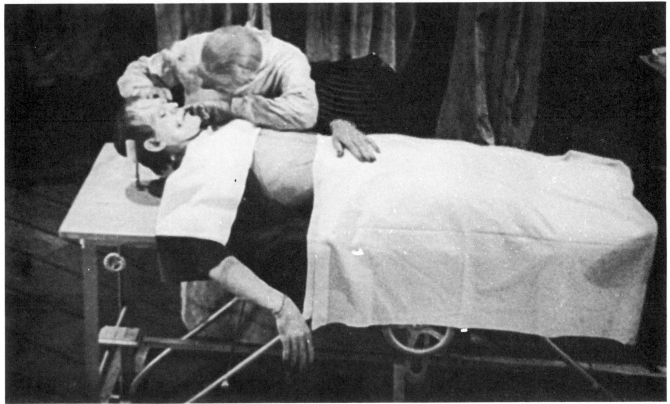

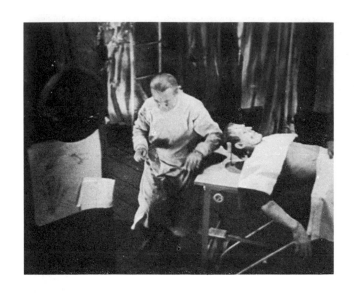

Patient still in state of anesthe...
...is for injection of 5:00–9:00 & 12

Tuesday 7 30 P.M.

Note increased resistance
Necessitating stronger and
more frequent injections.
However, will perform
dissection at once.

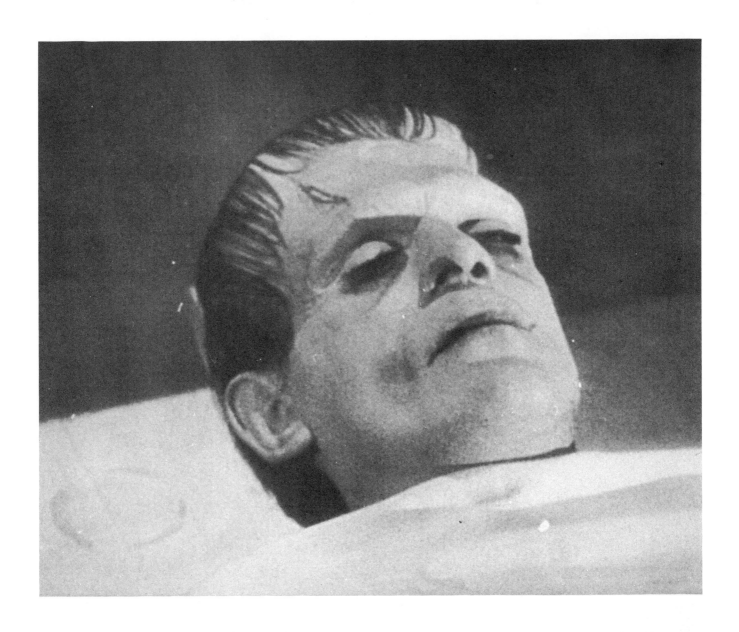

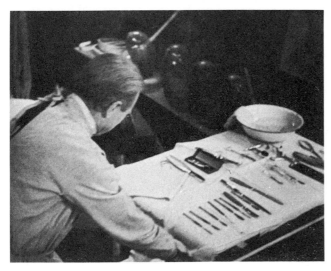

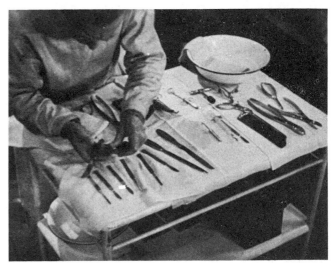

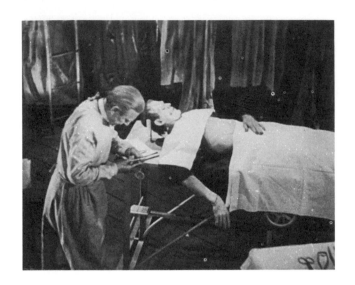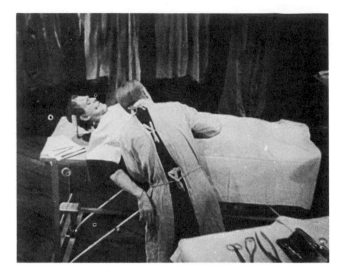

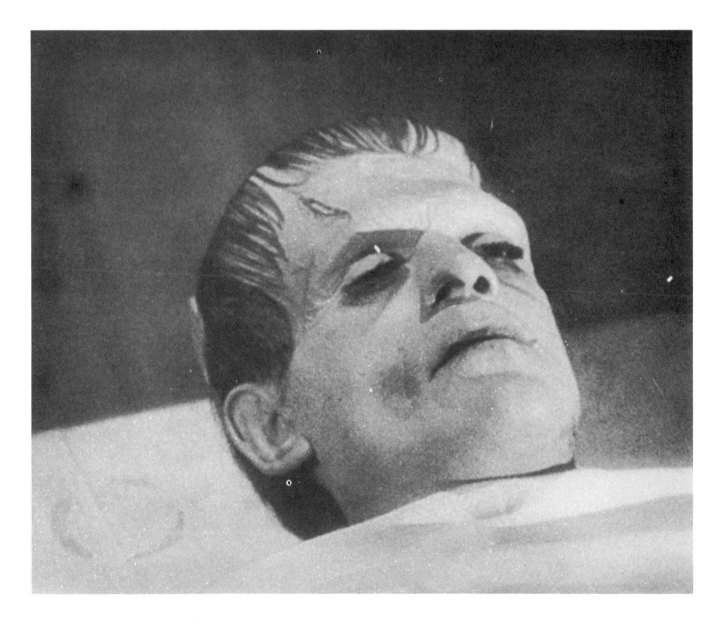

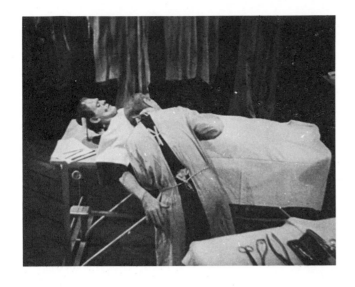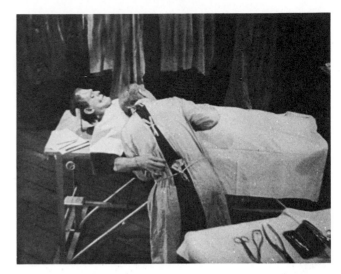

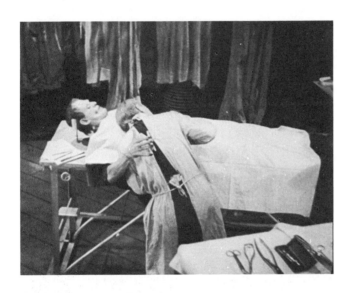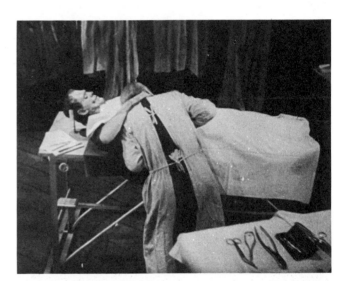

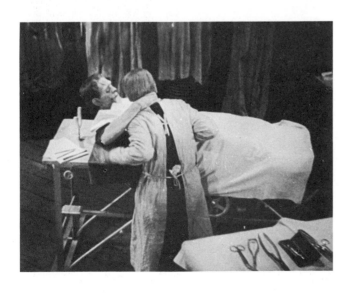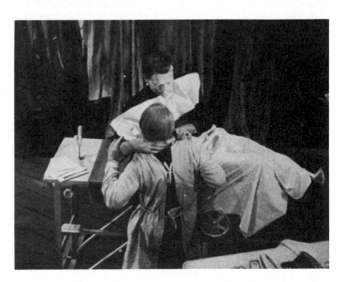

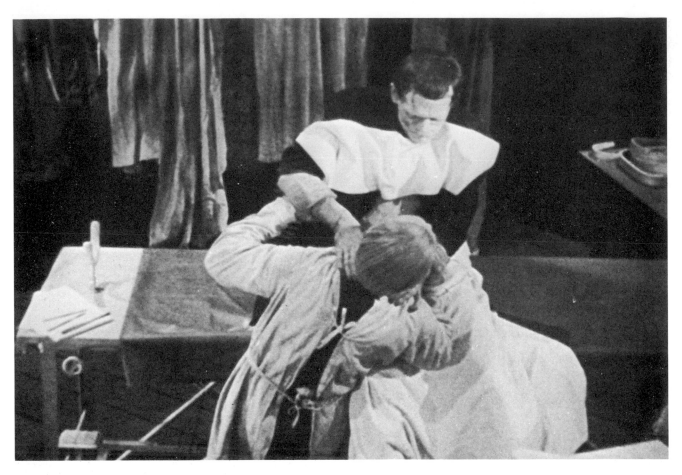

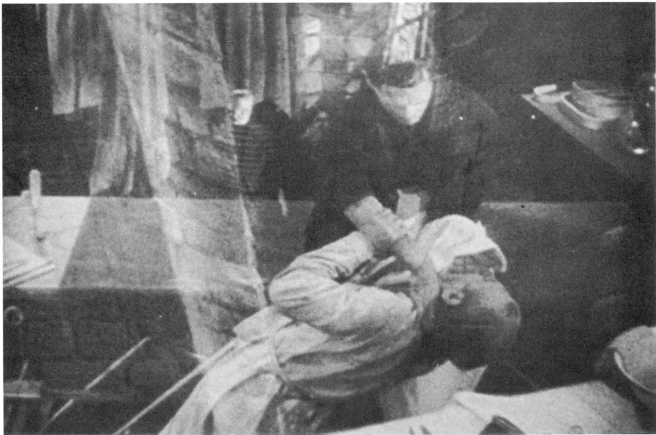

Frankenstein: It's like Heaven — being with you again.

Elizabeth: Heaven wasn't so far away all the time, you know.

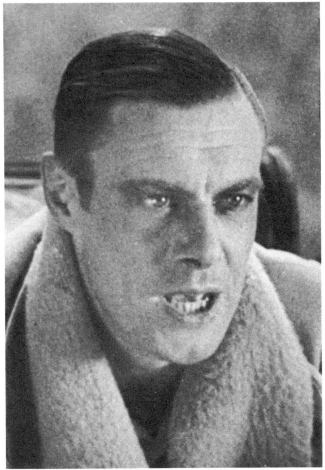

Frankenstein: I know, but I didn't realize it. My work — those horrible days and nights. I couldn't think of anything else.

Elizabeth: Henry, you're not to think of those things any more. You promised.

Frankenstein: All right, let's think about us. When will our wedding be?

Frankenstein: As soon as you like.

Baron: For three generations these orange blossoms have been worn at our weddings.

Baron: Your great-grandfather wore this, Henry. Looks as good as new now.
Frankenstein: Yes —

Baron: And here, here's one that will make the best man look still better.
Victor: Thank you, sir.

Baron: Thirty years ago I placed this on your mother's head, Henry. Today you will make me very happy by doing the same for Elizabeth. And I hope —

Baron: I hope in thirty years a youngster of yours will be carrying on the tradition. Now, now — how about a little drink, heh?

Baron: My — My grandfather bought this wine and laid it down — my grandmother wouldn't let him drink it. Bless her heart.

Baron: Here's your very good health. William are you all full?
Guest: Yes, Baron.

Baron: Well, come along. Here's health to a son of the House of Frankenstein.

Baron: Here's jolly good health to young Frankenstein.

Guests: To young Frankenstein!

Baron: Here, Heinz, give the women some champagne. This stuff's wasted on 'em.

Baron: Well, well, well, well — Go on, mop it up! Mop it up! It'll do you good.

Butler: The House of Frankenstein!

Servants: The House of Frankenstein!

Baron: Thank you. Now then, be off about your business.

Baron: Listen to 'em — listen to 'em. The boys and girls are happy I guess.

Baron: It's extraordinary how friendly you can make a lot of people on a couple of bottles of beer. Tomorrow they will all be fighting.

Man: No doubt.
Victor: They are calling for you, Baron.
Baron: Well, I suppose I'd better show myself.

Baron: Thank you all very much indeed. I am very pleased to see you all and I hope there's plenty of beer. If not —

Baron: There's plenty more where that came from.

Ludwig: You stay here Maria. I'll go take a look at my traps. And then we will go to the village and have a grand time, eh?

Maria: You won't be long, Daddy?

Ludwig: Oh no — no. If Hans comes by, tell him I'll be back soon.

Maria: Daddy, won't you stay and play with me a little while?

Ludwig: I'm too busy darling. You stay and play with the kitty, huh?

Ludwig: Goodbye. Be a good girl now.   **Maria:** Come on kitty.

Maria: Who are you?

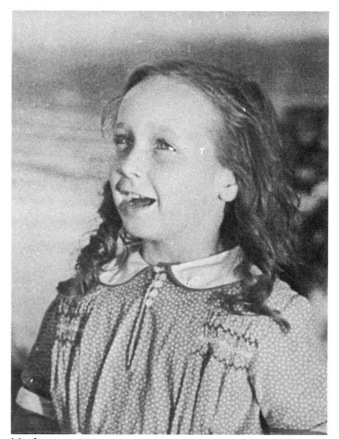

Maria: I am Maria.

Maria: Will you play with me?

Maria: Would you like one of my flowers?

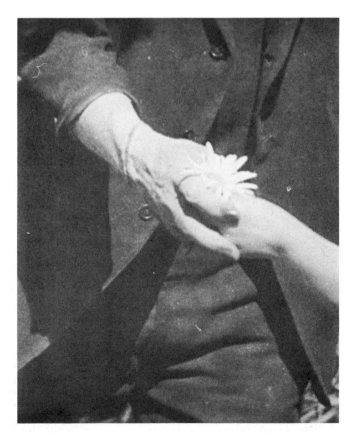

Maria: You have those — and I'll have these.

Maria: I can make a boat.

Maria: See how mine floats!

Elizabeth: Henry!

Frankenstein: Elizabeth!

Frankenstein: Oh, how lovely you look! But you shouldn't be here!
Elizabeth: I must see you for a morent.

182

Frankenstein: Why, what's the matter?

Elizabeth: Could you leave us for a moment?

Girl: Why of course.

Frankenstein: Oh, what is it?

Elizabeth: I'm so glad you're safe!

Frankenstein: Of course I'm safe. But you look worried. Is anything wrong?

Elizabeth: No — no, forget my foolishness. It was just a mood. There's nothing the matter.

Frankenstein: Of course there isn't.

Elizabeth: Oh Henry, I'm afraid, terribly afraid!

Elizabeth: Where's Doctor Waldman? Why is he late for the wedding?

Frankenstein: Oh, he's always late. He'll be here soon.

Elizabeth: Something is going to happen. I feel it. I can't get it out of my mind.

Frankenstein: You're just nervous. All the excitement and preparations.

Elizabeth: No — no — it isn't that. I've felt it all day.

Elizabeth: Something is coming between us. I know it. I know it!

Frankenstein: Sit down and rest. You look so tired.

Elizabeth: If I could just do something to save us from it!
Frankenstein: From what, dear? From what?

Elizabeth: I don't know.

Elizabeth: If I could just get it out of my mind!

Elizabeth: Oh I'd die if I had to lose you now, Henry!
Frankenstein: Lose me!

Frankenstein: Why I'll always be with you.

Elizabeth: Will you Henry?   Are you sure? I love you so.

Frankenstein: Sure.

Frankenstein: How beautiful you look.

Victor: Henry! Henry!
Elizabeth: What's that?

Elizabeth: What's that?

Victor: Henry! Dr. Waldman!

Frankenstein: What about Dr. Waldman?

Victor: Dr. Waldman!

Elizabeth: Henry, don't leave me!

 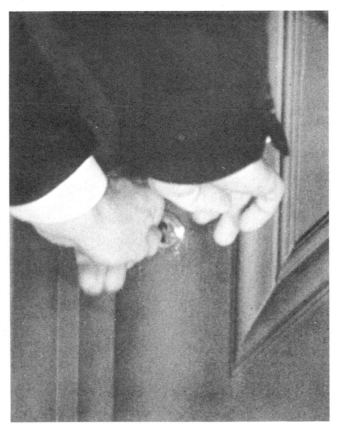

Elizabeth: Don't leave me!!

Frankenstein: No darling — you stay here.
Elizabeth: Henry! Henry!

Victor! Dr. Waldman's been murdered! In the tower. The monster!

Victor: He's been seen in the hills, terrorizing the mountainside.

Frankenstein: It's in the house! It's upstairs!

191

Frankenstein: It's in the cellar!

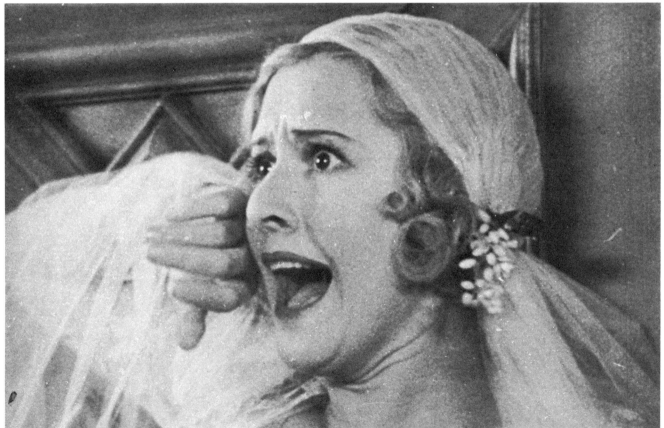

Frankenstein: It's Elizabeth!

Elizabeth: Don't let it come in here!

Frankenstein: No — no — no darling.
Elizabeth: Don't let it come here!
Frankenstein: It's all right.

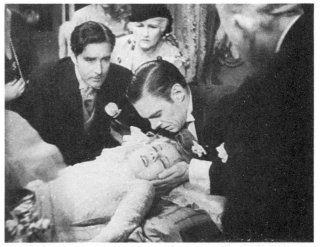

Elizabeth: Don't let it come here!
Frankenstein: It's all right darling — it's all right!

Girl: Oh look — it's Maria!

Burgomaster: Silence! Silence! What is it?
What is it?

Ludwig: Maria . . . she's drowned . . .

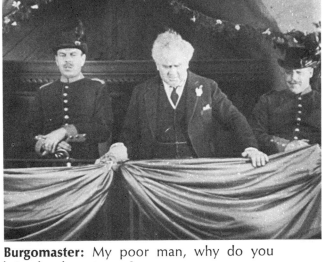

Burgomaster: My poor man, why do you bring her here to me?

Ludwig: But she's been murdered!

Burgomaster: Silence! I'll see that justice is done. Who is it?

Victor: How is Elizabeth now?
Frankenstein: I don't know, she's still in a daze. Just looks at me and says nothing. Oh it's maddening . . .

Victor: Easy old man, she'll be all right.
Frankenstein: Our wedding day.
Victor: Steady. The wedding will only be postponed a day, at most.

Frankenstein: A day, I wonder.
Victor: What do you mean?

Frankenstein: There can be no wedding while this horrible creation of mine is still alive! I made him with these hands and with these hands I will destroy him.

Frankenstein: I must find him.

Victor: I'll go with you.

Frankenstein: No, you stay here and look after Elizabeth.

Frankenstein: I leave her in your care . . . whatever happens . . . you understand? In your care . . .

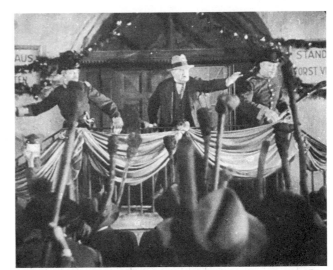

Guards: Quiet! Quiet!

Burgomaster: Silence!

Burgomaster: Ludwig. You will search the woods — Those are your group.

Burgomaster: Silence. Herr Frankenstein.

Burgomaster: You will take to the mountains — Those are your people.

Burgomaster: And search every ravine . . .

Burgomaster: . . . every crevice . . .

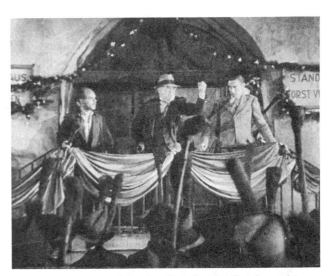

Burgomaster: . . . but the fiend must be found!

Burgomaster: Are you ready?
Mob: Yes!

Burgomaster: Light your torches and go . . .

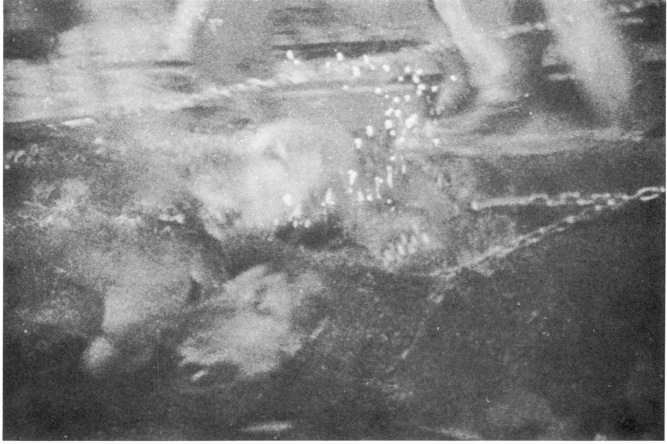

Burgomaster: STOP! Frankenstein . . .
Frankenstein . . . mountains . . .

Burgomaster: Lake party . . .

Burgomaster: This way . . .

Frankenstein: Come on boys . . . keep together . . .

Frankenstein: Now you search there . . . the rest come with me . . .

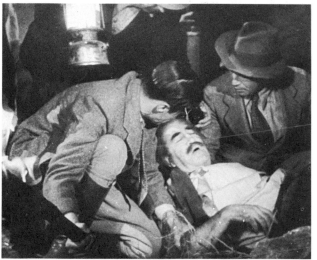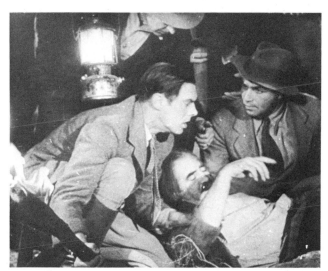

Frankenstein: Which way did he go, tell me? Tell me?

Man: Over there . . .

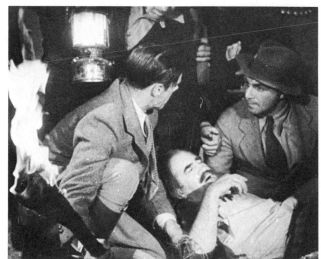

Frankenstein: You stay here and take care of him . . .

Frankenstein: The rest follow me . . .

Frankenstein: Come on . . .

Frankenstein: No . . . come back this way . . .

Ludwig: Herr Frankenstein . . . Herr Frankenstein . . . where are you?

Ludwig: I think he's up there . . . come on . . . follow me . . . quick . . .

Frankenstein: HELLO!...

Frankenstein: HELP! HELP!

Ludwig: Listen!

Ludwig: It's Frankenstein!

Burgomaster: That way . . .

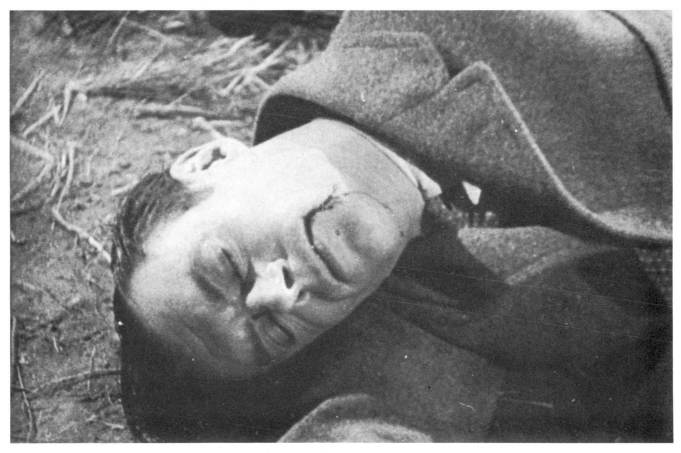

Burgomaster: Turn the hounds loose!

 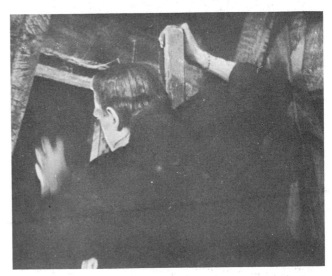

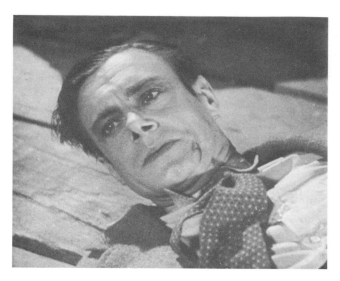

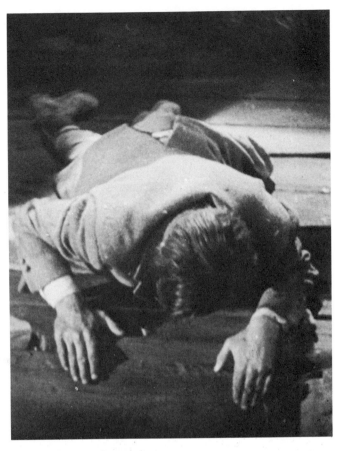

Burgomaster: There he is! There's the monster!

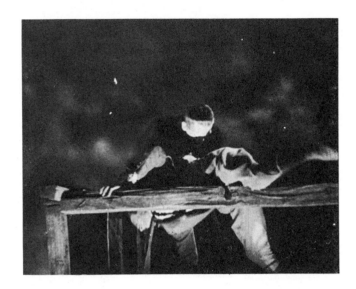

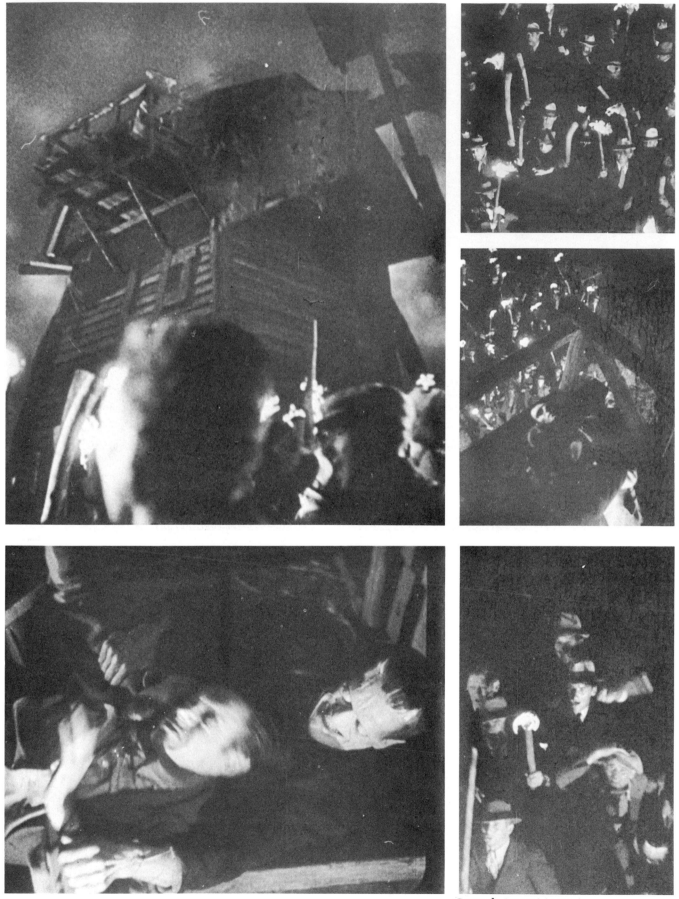

Crowd: Jump! Jump!

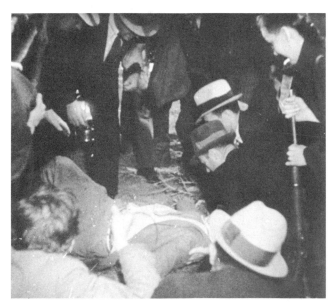

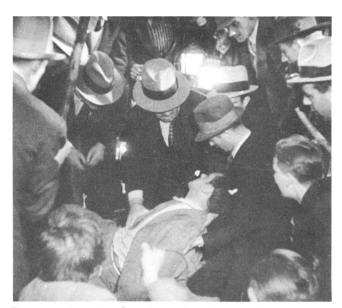

Men: He's alive! Yes!

Burgomaster: Frankenstein! Frankenstein!

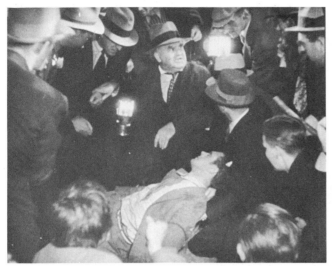

Burgomaster: Take him down to the village and let's get him home.

Man: Carefully, fellows! Stand back!

Men: Burn him out! Burn him out!

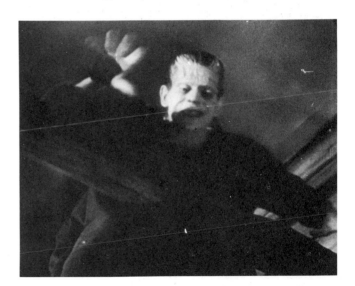

Men: Burn the mill! Burn it down!

Crowd: Burn the mill! Burn the mill!

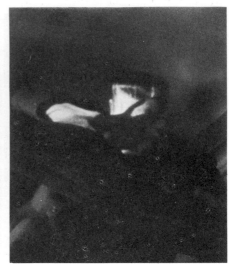

Crowd: Burn the mill! Burn the mill!

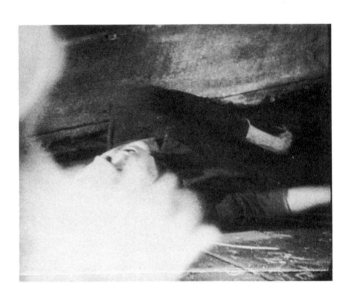

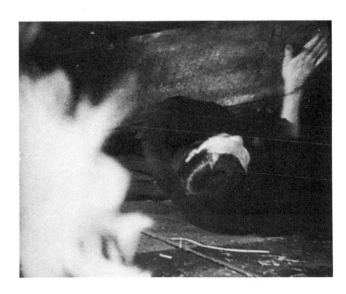

Housekeeper: Have you got 'em?
Maids: Yes.

Housekeeper: Well, come on! Hurry!

Maids: Hurry up!

Housekeeper: Well, go ahead and knock.

Baron: What — well, well — what's all this? What do you want, hey? What — what — what's this?

Housekeeper: If you please, Herr Baron, we thought that Mr. Henry could do with a draught of his great-grandmother's wine.

254

Baron: Fine old lady, my grandmother.

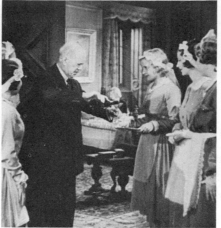

Baron: Very foreseeing of her to prevent my grandfather drinking this.

Baron: Mr. Henry doesn't need this.
Maids: No.

Baron: As I said before I say again — Here's — Here's to a son to the House of Frankenstein.

Maids: Indeed sir — we hope so, sir.

The End

It's a Universal Picture

A GOOD CAST IS WORTH REPEATING...

Henry Frankenstein ... COLIN CLIVE
Elizabeth ... MAE CLARKE
Victor Moritz ... JOHN BOLES
The Monster ... BORIS KARLOFF
Doctor Waldman ... Edward Van Sloan
Baron Frankenstein ... Frederick Kerr
Fritz ... Dwight Frye
The Burgomaster ... Lionel Belmore
Little Maria ... Marilyn Harris

DATE DUE

DEC 2 5 1995			